Animal Welfare & The Environment

An RSPCA Book

Edited by Richard D. Ryder

Foreword by Peter Singer

Duckworth
in association with the RSPCA

First published in 1992 by
Gerald Duckworth & Co. Ltd.
The Old Piano Factory
48 Hoxton Square, London N1 6PB

A catalogue record for this book is available
from the British Library

ISBN 0 7156 2403 2

Photoset in North Wales by
Derek Doyle & Associates, Mold, Clwyd.
Printed in Great Britain by
Redwood Press Ltd, Melksham

Contents

The Political Challenge

Conclusion

Foreword

Peter Singer

During the past two or three decades, two radical ideas have been gathering strength: animal liberation and the Green movement. They are distinct, but related. Both ideas can be seen as the logical extension of widely accepted and broadly based causes: animal welfare and concern for the environment. At first both animal liberation and Green politics seemed so extreme, so impractical, that they could only be taken up by a few free spirits on the margins of society. Now they have both broken through, and reached the point at which they can no longer be ignored.

Our daily newspapers provide ample evidence of the significance of these two ideas. The present volume, however, provides further evidence, of a different and more reflective kind. Not all contributors would describe themselves as either animal liberationists or as Greens, but even those who would not are reacting, in one way or another, to these two ideas. The book arises from a meeting; and much of the interest of its many excellent essays lies in the way in which the two streams of thought meet and are woven together in different ways by the various writers, each bringing their own perspective to the beginnings of what, I believe, will be a lasting marriage. (Though I have no illusions about the tranquillity of that particular relationship.)

It is noteworthy and commendable that the RSPCA should choose this theme to commemorate the 150th anniversary of its Royal title. The RSPCA has been a dominant presence in animal welfare for a very long time, but its relationship both to animal liberation and to the environmental movement has been less clear-cut. Its founders were, I would maintain, true animal liberationists. Many of them had first worked together in the Anti-Slavery Society. Lewis Gompertz, the second secretary of the society, who built it up to a position of considerable strength, was an ethical vegetarian who also refused to ride in horse-drawn vehicles. At some later stage, however, the RSPCA slipped away from these far-reaching ideals of its founders, and raised its voice only against 'wanton' or 'gratuitous' cruelty – without questioning all the suffering inflicted on animals in the name of such 'necessities' as meat production, which Gompertz and many others had demonstrated were not necessities at all. It is therefore especially welcome to see strong voices for animal liberation, such as Richard Ryder, Tom Regan and Andrew Linzey, contributing to this 150th anniversary RSPCA conference.

Both the animal liberation movement and the Greens question the right of our species to assume that *our* interests must always prevail. Animal liberationists want to extend the basic moral ideas of equality and rights – which we apply to all *human* beings – to animals as well. The Green movement is less easy to pin down to a philosophical position, but its supporters certainly would all reject the traditional Western belief that nature exists for us to exploit as best suits our immediate wants and desires.

To appreciate the importance of the common thread that links these two radical ideas, we have to remember that for virtually all of the history of Western civilisation, the right of human beings to trample over all other species on this planet, and over nature itself, has been taken for granted. A few dissident voices made themselves heard, but until very recent times they had little or no influence against the teaching of the ancient Hebrews that God had made Man the pinnacle of creation (with woman a step below) and given him Dominion over all the beasts. Nor could these dissidents unseat Aristotle, who for centuries was so pre-eminent that he was referred to simply as The Philosopher. Aristotle had taught that the less rational forms of life – plants and animals – exist for the sake of the more rational ones, humans. The Hebrew and Aristotelian strands of thought came together in Christianity. This religion's most influential interpreters – Paul, Augustine and Thomas Aquinas – denied that we have any duties at all to animals, plants or nature itself.

Now an alternative tradition is building, based on the two strands of animal liberation and radical environmentalism. These two strands are often mutually supportive in practice, although they are by no means identical in theoretical underpinnings. The environmentalist strand looks back to Henry Thoreau, who left the comforts of nineteenth-century city life to live out in the woods of Massachusetts by Walden Pond; and to Aldo Leopold, who wrote of 'the land ethic' in his *Sand County Almanac*. The other, the animal liberationist strand, has the late-eighteenth and early-nineteenth-century English utilitarian Jeremy Bentham as one source of inspiration; the social reformer Henry Salt, who lived about a century later, as another precursor; and some contemporary thinkers, well represented in this volume, are among those who have developed these ideas and helped to popularise them.

This alternative to the dominant Western view of nature will, if it is successful, bring far-reaching changes. The environmentalist aspect of it is already putting limits to development, placing barriers in the way of building dams or logging forests. The animal liberationist aspect has made fur socially unacceptable in Britain and the Netherlands, is forcing major changes in farming practices in several European nations, and is now persuading the major cosmetics companies to reconsider their practice of animal experimentation. Together, the two strands have given the world's great whales a respite (it is too early to say if it will prove to be more than that) from being slaughtered for commercial purposes.

In referring to the animal liberation and Green movements as making up an alternative to the dominant Western tradition, I have already suggested a partial answer to the question whether these two movements are in conflict. That question is, of course, central to this volume, and the reader should reserve judgment until all the essays have been read. Nevertheless, I shall state my own view here. It is that the two movements are pulling in the same direction, in so far as their opposition to human chauvinism is a central strand in both. Of course, there can be divergences on particular issues. The welfare of individual animals may conflict with environmental considerations. Here is one example. Rabbits were introduced into Australia by English settlers. They soon spread, and despite trapping, shooting, poisoning, the ripping up of warrens with tractors, the deliberate release of the myxomatosis virus and various other painful methods of destruction, they continue to exist in large numbers. There is little doubt that, in addition to eating grass that farmers want for more profitable animals, they also change Australia's flora and fauna, perhaps even contributing to serious soil erosion problems. Those primarily concerned with the environment favour getting rid of rabbits by any means that does not cause further environmental problems. On the other hand, animal liberationists are more concerned by the immense amount of suffering caused to rabbits by the attempt to exterminate them, and therefore oppose either all lethal methods of rabbit control, or at a minimum, all those – and it is most of them – which cause a slow and painful death.

This conflict between environmentalists and animal liberationists is the result of the original human stupidity of bringing rabbits to Australia, but it is a genuine conflict none the less. There are, however, possible solutions that could be satisfactory to all – for example, the development of methods of fertility control that could economically be applied to wild rabbit populations. In this sense the conflict is not inevitable or irreconcilable. It is a conflict at a relatively superficial level, below which there is something much more positive to be said. At the most fundamental level, genuine concern for animals and for the environment must pull us in the same direction. They are both striving to extend our concern beyond our own species; and after all, how could the interests of animals be satisfied without the preservation of the fragile layers of our planet on which all life depends?

Preface

This book is based on a conference held in Oxford to celebrate the 150th anniversary of the granting of the 'Royal' prefix to the RSPCA. It was the first major conference ever to address the important interface between animal protection and environmentalism. I am grateful to all the contributors for enabling us to publish.

The support of the members of the RSPCA Council, not least its Chairman, Joan Felthouse, has been invaluable, as has been the work of the RSPCA's staff, including Andrew Richmond, Michaela Miller, Ilona Billings, Tony Suckling and Michael Hall, and members of the Westminster Consortium.

Special thanks must go to Gavin Grant, Jerry Lloyd, Faith Fox-Holmes and Penny Merrett who have helped me in the preparation of the text. Finally, the assistance and enthusiasm of Dilys Vass, Jane Goodall, Andrew Linzey, Michael Shaw and, especially, Colin Haycraft and Deborah Blake have ensured fruition.

R.D.R.

Notes on Contributors

Donald M. Broom is Colleen MacLeod Professor of Animal Welfare in the Department of Clinical Veterinary Medicine at Cambridge.

Michael Fox is a Vice-President (Farm Animals & Bioethics) of the Humane Society of the United States of America. He has written over thirty books, among them *Farm Animals: Husbandry, Behavior and Veterinary Practice* (1984).

Edward Goldsmith is founder and publisher of *The Ecologist*. His publications include *The Social and Environmental Effects of Large Dams* (3 vols: 1984-90).

Jane Goodall is author of *My Friends the Chimpanzees* (1967) and *In the Shadow of Man* (1971).

Bryan Gould MP is the British Labour Party spokesperson on the Environment.

Sidney Holt is Scientific Advisor to the International Fund for Animal Welfare and a consultant to UNEP and Greenpeace.

Simon Hughes MP is the British Liberal Democrat spokesperson on the Environment.

James Kirkwood is Senior Veterinary Officer of the Zoological Society of London.

Andrew Linzey is Director of Studies at the Centre for the Study of Theology at the University of Essex. His most recent book is *Christianity and the Rights of Animals* (1987).

Mary Midgley was formerly Lecturer in Philosophy at the University of Newcastle-upon-Tyne. Her books include *Animals and Why They Matter* (1984).

Jonathon Porritt has been Director of Friends of the Earth and Chairman of the Ecology Party. His publications include *Seeing Green: The Politics of Ecology* (1984) and *The Coming of the Greens* (1988).

Tom Regan is Professor of Philosophy at North Carolina State

University. His publications include *The Case for Animal Rights* (1983).

Richard D. Ryder is a past Chairman of the RSPCA Council. His publications include *Victims of Science* (1975) and *Animal Revolution: Changing Attitudes Towards Speciesism* (1989).

James Serpell is Director of the Companion Animal Research Group at Cambridge. Recent publications include *In the Company of Animals* (1986).

Richard Simmonds MEP is a British Conservative Member of the European Parliament.

Peter Singer is Professor of Philosophy at Monash University, Melbourne. His best-known book is *Animal Liberation* (1975).

Anthony Suckling is Chief Scientific Officer of the RSPCA.

Ian Swingland is Director of the Durrell Institute of Conservation and Ecology at the University of Kent. He was recently Chairman of the RSPCA's Wild Animals Advisory Committee.

Patrick Wall is Professor in the Cerebral Functions Research Group of University College & Middlesex School of Medicine, University of London. He is co-author, with Ronald Melzack, of *The Challenge of Pain* (1982).

John Webster is Professor in the Department of Animal Husbandry at the University of Bristol.

David Wilkins is Chief Veterinary Officer of the RSPCA.

Introduction

Richard D. Ryder

Since the 1960s there has been a huge international upsurge of interest in our animate and inanimate environment – a Green revolution in thought. Like someone at the end of a busy week who sits down and, for the first time for days, has time to look around, so the affluent world has begun to observe and reflect upon its surroundings. Two main strands of this new thoughtfulness are apparent – one is a concern with the well-being of the other animals with whom we share the planet, and the other is a more general interest in the whole environment. Strangely, perhaps, these two strands of the Green revolution have remained somewhat apart, so that many organisations and individuals concern themselves exclusively with one or the other but not with both. This raises some questions of sociological, political and moral interest. What is the relationship between animal welfare and general environmentalism? To what extent do the two fields coincide in terms of political objectives, history and ethical foundations? There is clearly a need to address these questions and to explore the areas of overlap and divergence.

In recognition of this need, the Royal Society for the Prevention of Cruelty to Animals (RSPCA) – the world's oldest and largest animal welfare body – organised an international Conference at Oxford in August 1990 to celebrate the 150th anniversary of the granting of the Society's 'Royal' prefix by Queen Victoria. Those who addressed the Conference are among the leaders of the two movements and, as campaigners, politicians, philosophers and scientists, they approach the subject from a wide range of viewpoints.

Although to some the link between animal protection and environmentalism seems an obvious one, to others it is not. Why should there exist this divergence of opinion?

There may be historical answers to such a question. A worship of trees and rocks and animals is, of course, older than history itself, and so is the human exploitation of them. But as, with increased technology, humankind gained the mastery of nature, so the exploitative approach overtook the religious. During the Renaissance the subjugation of nature to the human species became a matter of pride and, with industrialisation, increasingly destructive. All things, so it was argued, had been created for the benefit of humankind. Yet, over the ages, there had always been voices raised against such arrogance, and in the eighteenth century they become more numerous. The educated classes of Northern Europe began to acknowledge the beauty and significance of the natural world and, slowly, attitudes changed towards animals and the countryside. At the turn of the century British politicians, for example, began their attempts to protect animals through the law; in 1822 they had their first such legislative success and, two years later, the Society was born which was to become the RSPCA.[1]

Although Britain led the way with the formal protection of animals, this was less obviously the case with the protection of the inanimate environment. Why? I believe it was because the word of the major landowners in Britain was already tantamount to law and, although some did develop their land industrially, the dominant ethic was one of preservation; the country gentleman not only planted trees, planned parks and preserved copses, hedges and streams, but also fiercely defended his land against railways and any other unsightly development. Britain was not only the first industrialised nation, it was also the first to discover the antidote to industry – the beauty of an unspoiled countryside. Some of the motives for such preservation were, undoubtedly, agricultural and sporting, but it would be wrong to exaggerate these aspects. The ideals of the country gentleman and lady were ones of refinement; they stocked their libraries with books of natural history, their gardens with flowers and their parks with fine trees.

Thus, in Britain, an unarticulated but powerful environmentalism existed from the late eighteenth century on. In America this was not so; in much of the country there was no traditional and wealthy landowning class to restrain development. On the contrary, the prevailing ethic was that of the pioneer who still saw his duty as the conquest and exploitation of nature. It was not only his duty – his survival depended upon it; the timber, the gold and the buffalo had to be converted into food for himself and his children. The reaction against this unrestrained development, which came in the mid-nineteenth century with writers such as Henry David Thoreau, John Muir and George Perkins Marsh, set the pattern for American environmentalism.[2] Particularly on the West coast this has always concentrated upon conservation and the preservation of trees, mountains, air and water, rather than on the protection of animals from cruelty. On the East coast the anti-cruelty laws and societies followed the British precedent more closely and began to flourish in the 1860s after the end of the Civil War. The emphases of the American and British movements are thus complementary. The British had established a *de facto* protection of the land but had openly to campaign and legislate against cruelty to animals – a cruelty for which Britain had been internationally renowned in earlier centuries.[1] The Americans, on the other hand, with less emphasis upon cruel sports but with an entrepreneurial tradition of massive and unrestrained destruction of forests, mining of mountainsides and damming of rivers, had to campaign explicitly for their protection. As a result, America led the world in the establishment of great natural parks – Yellowstone in 1872, the Adirondacks in1885 and Yosemite in 1890.

On the continent of Europe, too, environmentally-minded writers and campaigners appeared during the nineteenth century. Laws against cruelty to animals were passed in Germany in the 1830s, and the first German animal welfare society was inaugurated in Stuttgart in 1837. Switzerland and the Scandinavian countries were not far behind.[1, pp. 167-9] On the environmental side two distinct strands of nineteenth-century thought emerged:[3] on the one hand that of the economic environmentalists, such as the Russian, Prince Peter Kropotkin, who initiated the modern interest in the conservation of energy, soil, land and other natural resources, and on the other the biological strand, exemplified in the work of the German, Ernst Haeckel, who coined the word 'ecology' in 1866, defining it as 'the science of relations between organisms and their environment'.

As regards animals, it is interesting to note that the two figures now regarded as the outstanding early environmental pioneers on either side of the Atlantic, Ernst Haeckel and Henry Thoreau, united their concerns for the environment with a deep compassion for other living creatures, Thoreau seeing a muskrat simply as 'a different sort of man – that is all'[4] and Haeckel regarding humans and non-humans as equal parts of a unified nature towards which he expressed his reverence. After Thoreau and Haeckel, however, environmentalists showed much less interest in the well-being of animals, and the two movements drifted further apart. Nor did many of the leading animal welfarists show much interest in environmentalism. They were often active in other causes such as the anti-slavery movement or the campaigns to improve the treatment of women and children,[5] but environmentalism seems to have passed them by. Is there a psychological or sociological explanation for this, or are the two movements naturally distinct?

There seem, from the mid-nineteenth century, to be at least seven main motives for environmentalism, each producing a slightly different outlook. We can call these seven outlooks the *thrifty*, the *aesthetic*, the *scientific*, the *historic*, the *health-conscious*, the *compassionate* and the *mystical*. The first position characteristically emphasises the need to save energy or other natural resources (including animals) so that they remain available for human use. The second is concerned chiefly about the beauty of the countryside and its wildlife, and of historic buildings. The third wishes to preserve things for scientific study, and the fourth because they are historic. The fifth is concerned about threats to human health posed by radiation or chemical pollution. The sixth, the compassionate, is anxious not to hurt things. Finally, the seventh is a variant of this compassionate position where the environmentalist argues poetically or mystically for the one-ness of nature and attributes 'value' to sentient and insentient alike.

It can be seen that all these positions, except the last two, are speciesist and anthropocentric: that is to say, they seek some advantage to the human species as their ultimate aim and are not concerned for things in the environment for their own sake. An environmentalist typically combines a number of these positions and can, sometimes bewilderingly, move from one to another in quick succession! Basically, however, we find four ethical positions – a concern for *sentient* creatures, a concern for all *life* (including trees and other vegetation usually considered to be insentient), a concern for *all natural features* of the environment (including inanimate features such as rocks and rivers and mountains) and a concern which also includes some *human-made things*, such as old buildings.

The third position derives some of its popularity from a twentieth-century writer, Aldo Leopold, who is little known in Britain but widely regarded in America. Leopold subordinated the importance of the individual to what he called 'the *biotic community*'. It was, he said in 1948, important to preserve 'the integrity, stability and beauty' of this community, although he did not seem to be clear, in his own mind, exactly what he meant by this or why it was important. Nevertheless his influence has been considerable in America and, in some circles, has led to the questionable view that an ethic for rocks and mountains is somehow a more *advanced* position than one based upon suffering. In general it can be seen that environmentalists can differ from animal rightists in being concerned with species rather than individuals, with value rather than pain, and with human interests rather than the interests or rights of all.

From the 1960s onwards the Green Movement began to escalate.[1,5] In Britain, once again, it was the animal rights issue which came into prominence, with activist campaigns against bloodsports, animal experimentation,[6] and factory-farming, and the publication of serious anti-speciesist literature by the informal 'Oxford Group'.[7] America and the rest of Europe followed the British lead a few years later. In America, again, the early emphasis of the new Green revolution was not upon animal liberation but general environmental protection; Friends of the Earth and Greenpeace were both started in 1969, crossing the Atlantic to London a few years later. Earlier, originating in Britain, the World Wildlife Fund had concentrated upon the conservation of wildlife, and the International Fund for Animal Welfare, founded in Canada, had begun its long crusade against the killing of seals, using welfare as well as conservation arguments. During the economic recessions of the early 1980s and early 1990s British public and media interest slightly declined in all matters Green. Yet the movements have had a growing underlying appeal. Indeed the sheer fashionableness of Green issues seems recently to have brought into the movement people whose backgrounds are rather far removed from it. Agriculturalists, hunters and foresters, all with a basically *exploitative* approach, now appear in Green apparel as 'environmental scientists' or 'ecologists'. But old habits die hard and one can find such people calling for the felling of trees which do not grow straight, the mass destruction of species which they label 'pests' (sometimes in the interests of species 'variety') and, most strangely of all, the extermination of animals or plants which are deemed to be 'foreign'. Such eco-racism is now well-established in Britain, as one sees in the co-ordinated destruction of one of nature's most beautiful creations – the rhododendron. Similarly, animal welfare is also being populated by veterinarians and biologists whose views do not seem so far removed from those who factory-farm or vivisect. Should we not welcome such recruits? Will the genuine environmental and animal welfare ethics survive such apparent converts?

Politically speaking, environmentalism has its occasional conflicts with animal welfare as, for example, in arguments about the necessity for killing certain wild animals in order to protect flora; such a case is the killing of red deer in parts of Scotland in order to allow the regeneration of ancient pine forest. Furthermore, various environmental policies clearly have been shown to be in conflict among themselves. Should beautiful exotics be extirpated in order to preserve more traditional plant life? Here aesthetic values conflict with 'heritage' values. Should the construction of tidal barrages be allowed in order to produce clean and renewable energy if such work threatens birdlife? Here anti-pollution and fossil-fuel conservation arguments clash with wildlife conservation. Should unsightly windmill farms be constructed on majestic cliff tops? Should the scientific interest take precedence over the compassionate or historic? Often environmental protection policy becomes a matter of choice between conflicting advantages. In Africa the choice sometimes seems to be between conserving nonhumans (such as elephants) and allowing indigent humans a chance fully to exploit the land. Should overcrowded wildlife populations be culled for their own benefit? The benefits of tourism, both psychological and commercial, are often set against shorter-term and more concrete human benefits, and indeed raise another question. Should wildlife habitats be left wild, or should humankind intervene in order to 'manage' them? Should some species (the photogenic, perhaps, or the rare, or the scientifically interesting) be protected from other species? Should the jungle be sanitised or Disneyfied? If so, to what extent? Should 'nasty' species (scorpions, poisonous snakes, tsetse flies) be exterminated? Should humans protect prey from predators? Should carnivores be persecuted and herbivores favoured? How far should humankind intervene to help sick and injured wildlife? Should there be a 'health service' for wild animals? Do humans have a moral duty to roam the pampas looking for injured mammals, reptiles or insects in order to give them treatment? The idea of widespread veterinary care for wild animals has, until recent times, seemed rather far-fetched. Yet, unless one is a speciesist, there is a strong moral argument for some such active intervention.

The plan of this book is based closely upon the program of the Oxford Conference itself. Historical and philosophical chapters are followed by scientific and political. Not all contributors to this symposium are true believers, and their misgivings and occasional scepticism add, I hope, some spice to the debate. Not every view, of course, reflects those of the RSPCA itself.

Of one thing I am certain – environmental protection and animal welfare are fields which are gaining in both academic and political stature, and the future will see them accorded their proper and rightful places in academia and government. Above all, these are ethical questions. As old values crumble, the human animal yearns for a new morality, and one that slots securely into the modern experience. We are, surely, seeing a significant moral revolution, perhaps the most significant there has ever been; the extension of morality beyond the human species. We are doing in moral terms what

Galileo did in cosmological – dethroning our own kind. We are also establishing a millennial morality on its only sure foundation – a respect for the rights of *all* things which suffer pain.

References

1. Richard D. Ryder: *Animal Revolution: Changing Attitudes Towards Speciesism*, Blackwell, 1989
2. Roderick Frazier Nash: *The Rights of Nature: A History of Environmental Ethics*, University of Wisconsin Press, 1989
3. Anna Bramwell: *Ecology in the Twentieth Century: A History*, Yale University Press, 1989
4. Henry D. Thoreau: *Journal*, quoted in Jon Wynne-Tyson, *The Extended Circle: An Anthology of Humane Thought*, Cardinal, 1990, p. 538.
5. Richard D. Ryder: 'The Struggle against Speciesism' in David Paterson and Richard D. Ryder (eds), *Animal Rights – A Symposium*, Centaur Press, 1979
6. Richard D. Ryder: *Victims of Science*, Davis-Poynter, 1975, 2nd edition, Centaur Press, 1983
7. Stanley and Roslind Godlovitch, and John Harris (eds), *Animals, Men and Morals*, Gollancz, 1971.

1. The Development of Green Awareness

Jonathon Porritt

This conference is a very important initiative. The RSPCA has brought together representatives of, and people interested in, two profound movements which I believe will have a great influence on the way the human species evolves. I cannot go into detail on the issues which members of one of those movements – the environmentalists – hold to be most vital. If I started on a catalogue of what is going wrong with the world, let alone what we might do to put it right, there would be no end.

I would like instead to consider some of the attitudes and concerns that *underlie* those issues. I shall take as my starting point a television programme I imagine many of you will have seen recently. This featured the Worldwide Fund for Nature and claimed to reveal degrees of incompetence, if not corruption, within that organisation, which made it no longer worthy of the support of the Great British and international public. It was a disgraceful piece of television, in as much as it failed completely to set one point of view against another so that genuine truth could emerge. It was simplistic, it was an insult to many of those people taking part, it was ruthlessly edited and – it was fascinating! But what Roger Cook and his researchers entirely failed to do was to use the interesting current developments within WWF to highlight a crucial debate of which we are all a part – namely the *values* that should now guide the work we do in our respective movements, and how to make those values germane and relevant to people the world over.

Joan Felthouse indicated in her introductory comments that many members of the Animal Welfare Movement dislike being referred to as 'bunny huggers'. And yet, of course, that derogatory, throw-away term of abuse does sum up a position that some people choose to adopt in defence of the natural world and its species. On the other hand, there are those who are hopelessly compromised who believe that the only means by which we can achieve successful conservation is by bringing on board local people, and working together with them to achieve the most harmonious interaction between humans and wildlife. I shall come back to those value-laden questions later.

The Worldwide Fund for Nature is, of course, just one part of a huge international Green Movement, in which we have seen massive increases in the number of supporters over the past few years. In trying to sum up what this Green Movement is you need to distinguish between two important polarities, or tendencies. The first is the 'light green' tendency. The light greens by and large believe that the system of which we are all a part is perfectible, that it could be reformed in such a way as to create a sustainable, environmentally friendly way of living. At the other end of the spectrum are the 'dark greens', who believe essentially that the system is inherently corrupt and unsustainable, and that any attempts to ameliorate its impact on the natural world are utterly forlorn. What they advocate is the wholesale transformation of the system so that something quite different can emerge.

These two directions or shades of opinion are not necessarily as starkly polarised as may appear. Indeed the interesting thing about the Green Movement is its continuity – the fact that all the different shades of opinion are linked in a single green swathe. The light-greens themselves are variegated, ranging from respectable Establishment bodies like the National Trust and the RSPB at one end to the more radical organisations like Greenpeace and Friends of the Earth at the other. And then the dark-greens are by no means united in forming a simple statement of what it is to be an out-and-out green. Some feel that politics is the best route, others that politics is completely irrelevant and that we need instead a spiritual revolution.

I suspect that as I map out some of those tendencies they will sound familiar to many people, for in some respects the distinction between light-greens and dark-greens is a mirror image of the distinction between animal *welfare* activists and animal *rights* activists. Essentially light-greens and welfarists are in the business of compromising, and compromising with pride, as they feel that this is the most effective way of making progress in our society. Those on the dark green or rights side of the debate voice varying degrees of absolutism with an equal amount of pride, because they feel that the stating of and defence of those absolutes is the only means by which to reform the system. Yet, despite such similarities, the Environment Movement and the Animal Welfare Movement remain quite separate in the way they proceed. It was not really until the emergence of a more holistic Green politics four or five years ago that we began to see how powerful are the connections between those two apparently separate sets of concerns. It is probably fair to say that some environmentalists have been careful not to over-identify with those involved in the animal welfare or animal rights movements. On many occasions I have heard environmentalists say that they do not wish to be 'tarred by the same brush' which has so comprehensively covered some extremists in the Animal Rights Movement and which has brought that movement into disrepute. I have also heard many environmentalists argue with passion that the cause of animal rights is subsidiary to the cause of protecting the environment, and that one will only follow from the other. I have also heard people involved in the Animal Rights Movement argue exactly the same thing the other way round!

But fundamentally, of course, there is a massive overlap between the two movements in terms both of the issues and of the values and philosophical concerns that give our work any meaning at all. And both movements are in the throes of similar internal debates between those who believe that a step-by-step, incremental approach to reform is the best means to make progress and those who believe in a far more absolutist confrontational approach.

At the root of the debate there lies one real question that every organisation in either movement has to confront: does gradualism genuinely mitigate the damaging behaviour of society, or does it subtly and insidiously reinforce that behaviour by subscribing to its basic value? To what extent is co-operation with the system compromised within the system? To what extent are recent developments indicators of a fundamental betrayal of a different value system? The success of the Green Movement over the last few years has left that rather uncomfortable question hanging in the air. Very few environmentalists would choose to engage in a debate about the extent to which they had either succeeded or sold out. Most of them are riding high on a feeling that all politicians and most of the media now put the environment at or near the top of the political agenda. Most of them do feel that they have succeeded in bringing on board the majority of people in a country such as this to support their claims. Let us look a little more closely at how that success has been achieved and examine the standards by which it can be judged.

The first significant point is that over the last decade environmentalists have learnt how to use science much more authoritatively, to bring a new professional competence to their campaigns. It is extremely rare now to find environmental organisations out-manoeuvred by scientists, or by corporate or other interests using science as a weapon against them. That has made a huge difference, and in terms of the response to the issues among so-called 'decision-makers' it is this increasing ability on the part of the environmental organisations to marshal good accurate evidence behind them that has begun to tilt the balance of opinion in their favour. Secondly, environmentalists are now extremely nimble at arguing the whole notion of self-interest as the strongest justification for environmental protection; indeed it has become something of an art form to demonstrate that measures to protect the environment are essentially of value to human beings and that this is the best reason for their implementation that there could possibly be. But we need to look closely at such a rhetorical tool. It brings us back to the old calculus of human happiness, back to the rationalisations by which different measures and patterns of investment are justified *purely* in terms of their direct or indirect benefit to *ourselves*. Environmental organisations have worked that one to the hilt. If you look, for example, at the case that has been made for the protection of the rainforest, you will find that it is peppered with every conceivable argument. But eventually the arguments all boil down to the fact that it is more economic to harvest the rainforest sustainably than clear-fell it in the idiotic way we have been doing until now, and that this is of immense benefit to us, the human species, because of the maintenance of that genetic diversity which will cure all sorts of dreadful diseases in the future. The rainforest is also held to be useful to us because it will help to mitigate the worst impacts of global warming. Unapologetic utilitarianism of the old kind. Save the rainforest because it is good for us.

The 'rational' and utilitarian planks of the success of the Green Movement are also interesting because of the burden they place on the importance of good science. Environmentalists have ceased to feel any degree of confidence in talking about emotion. Indeed the notion that one has emotions is now deeply suspect! The idea that we might feel, that we might be angry, that we might care, that we might even have what are disparagingly known as 'gut feelings' rather than hard scientific evidence, is held to be something of a problem if you are an environmentalist on the road to success. Instead we have quite enthusiastically lapsed into a chronic dualism where the whole emotional side of the human psyche has been suppressed. We have simultaneously slipped back into a compromising embrace with the very form of instrumental utilitarianism which got the world into such a mess in the first place: that things are of value because they are of value to us, not because they are of value in themselves.

I have come to believe that the dualism and utilitarianism that now lie behind what many environmentalists are doing today poses a threat that most environmentalists don't even begin to understand. The problem is that it has the effect of actually *reinforcing* alienation, leaving room for that disjunction from the natural world which allows certain scientists to behave with inconceivable cruelty in their laboratories, which allows workers in slaughter houses to treat animals as if they simply had no rights or feelings at all, which allows people to justify all manner of exploitation, as if there were no moral obligations or injunctions upon us whatsoever. That, I think, explains so much of the anger and the deep sense of hurt that many people in the Animal Rights Movement and the Environment Movement feel. They see those practitioners of cruelty in their laboratories, those operators in the slaughter houses, as only the most extreme example of an omnipresent form of alienation which unfortunately embraces almost all human beings today.

To me, therefore, the most exciting thing about the Environment Movement at this point is the ethical, moral and spiritual challenge it is raising up against those old utilitarian and dualistic values. We see this in the increasing influence of the new Ecology Movement, in the power of the Gaia theory, in the efforts of established religions to come to terms with their part in dealing with these issues; and much more humbly, but much more universally, we see it in the increased attention that so many of us are now paying to the ways we celebrate the beauty and diversity of life on Earth. That spiritual dimension I believe to be of pivotal importance; indeed I believe it to be the soul of the Green Movement today.

And here we come to the crunch – the core of the paradox. In order to allow that spiritual dimension to breathe, in order to allow it to work its healing, transformative way, we have no option but to operate in the world as it is, and to operate as gradualists. I reach that sorry conclusion after years of involvement in one environmental organisation or another, and I defend such a position for two reasons. The first is unavoidable pragmatism. That, essentially, is how the system works. It is boring to have to say that (it actually makes me twitch even as I do!), but it is no good pretending that it works in any other way, because it simply doesn't.

That does not mean that we have to throw the baby out with the bath water. Within the Environmental Movement there is a useful, indeed a symbiotic, relationship between the absolutists and the pragmatists. But we do all recognise that without that balance, in certain instances, absolutism can easily spill over into extremism. At that point, extremism almost always tends to become counter-productive. When anger turns to violence we can see people actually withdrawing, actually pulling back, from a sense of involvement in the ideas and values that we are putting forward. In very few cases should human beings be tempted to fight violence with violence. The utter incongruity of seeking to protect the natural world, both creatures and habitat, by threatening the well-being or life of one part of that natural world in the name of another is mind-boggling; such violence is foolish, cowardly and morally indefensible.

The second reason why I feel that gradualism is the only means by which we shall achieve any kind of new vision for society and for the natural world has everything to do with the workings of democracy. You cannot force people to protect trees, wetlands, top soil, water or indeed other species. You can only encourage and teach and cajole and provide incentives and gradually open the closed minds of the dominant species on Earth today. One can, in short, only enhance the evolution of the human spirit to the point where such a vision is genuinely embraced. If we accept that as a precondition of change, we have to accept that those changes must come about democratically. If we accept *that*, we have to accept the slow, tortuous, frustrating business of working and being effective within that democracy, however inadequate it may be.

Now this, I think, is where approaches to the issues begin to diverge, and where the debate about tactics begins to take over. For my part, I have said that I think it is possible to justify gradualist, incremental tactics as a means of bringing about lasting change. But the really pertinent question is *why* are we engaging in gradualistic, incremental tactics, or indeed any tactics at all? What is the motivation behind our involvement? It is in the answer to that question, I believe, that the solution to the paradox can be found.

The debate should *not* endlessly be about tactics, it becomes self-defeating to go on and on and on wrangling about tactics when it is the motivation behind those tactics that holds the key. It is here that the goal of developing a different *vision*, for locating a different set of values, becomes pre-eminent – because with that different vision, with a determination to create a new set of values which recognises intrinsic value in all living creatures, we can properly inform and inspire a programme that works, albeit a gradualist one! Without that vision, you can guarantee that every single environmental and animal welfare organisation will be bought off and co-opted by a system that does not care a jot about the natural world and its creatures. Without those different values, without that recognition of intrinsic value, without a different approach to an interpretation of stewardship, without a truly spiritual understanding of our relationship with the rest of life on Earth, both the Environment Movement and the Animal Welfare Movement are, in my opinion, condemned to irrelevance.

That of course puts a heavy burden on all of us, constrained as we are by having to work in underfunded, hard-pressed organisations pitted against monstrously powerful vested interests, and struggling often against ignorance and indifference at the same time. But I think it is reasonable as well as constructive to allude to the possibility that the human spirit is indeed evolving, that we are gradually 'widening the circle of compassion', moving away from the narrower, more self-interested, more aggressive forms of social organisation to embrace the concept of one world in which we do indeed see ourselves as members of one human family. But then, of course, there is one step beyond that which most people would find an even greater challenge: to widen the circle so that we see ourselves not only as one part of one *human* family, but of the family of all life on Earth.

And that is also, I believe, where the challenge to this conference really lies. How can we actually articulate that sense of a broader vision? How can we bring that message home in such a way that more and more people can locate their own individual efforts within it?

2. The Human Impact on Wildlife and the Environment

Ian Swingland

Since the beginning, humans have used the available natural resources for their survival; to feed and house their family, and to keep warm. As human populations increased villagers had to go further afield in search of food. This was undoubtedly one of the stimuli for the development of agriculture, selected agricultural cultivars, and the keeping of domestic stock. The wear on horses' teeth from thirty thousand years ago clearly shows signs commensurate with what we know as crib-biting and confirms that they were domesticated even then.

With the exponential explosion of human populations in the last hundred years the natural resources on which such societies traditionally depended have been under increasing pressure both from the indigenous people and from foreigners who had little thought or concern for practising sustainable harvesting. The foreigners were preoccupied with profit and getting as much as they could as quickly as possible.

These transient colonialists dictated their needs, and the local populations in general complied. For many indigenes this meant that their once dependable resources were whittled away to the point of non-sustainability. Even after the departure of the foreigners, resources which were still in plentiful supply at that time were under increasing pressure from the by now much increased local populations and the new way of doing things inherited from their colonial masters. The profit incentive was instilled in what used to be purely a subsistence mentality of only taking what was needed.

Development and international aid are frequently misguided in inception, disastrous in execution and catastrophic for the local people. Zambians in the Kafue National Park take fry from the tributaries of the Kafue River using Government-issued mosquito nets because they can't fish the main river for adult fish as the new Lake created by the hydro-electric dam did not have the standing trees removed before flooding. Images of NIMBY and the national interest versus the local interest arise. It would be more acceptable if the dam made electricity, but it is silted up because the water analysis got muddled up and the river is much siltier than was originally expected.

Today the rate of increase in food production has exceeded the rate of increase in the total world population. But in the developing world the rate of increase in food production has been exceeded by the rate of increase of the population, and now there is not enough food being produced in the developing world for the local population. All the excess food is in the wrong places or in the wrong hands. The locals are turning back to wildlife and natural resources to survive.

Most significantly, attitudes to animal welfare and conservation have changed radically in the last forty years to the point that they are among the most important six issues for the future and will dominate debate. What are the other five? They are:

health & pollution
food
continuing education
economic exploitation
and an individual's integrity and quality of life

The Victorians parcelled up Africa with the help of the other Europeans. Straight lines were drawn on maps by Whitehall bureaucrats to represent the borders of countries, and concerns for the disappearing wildlife were manifest in the establishment of National Parks and reserves to protect wildlife and in the expulsion of the villagers from their traditional homes to be re-settled outside the borders of a park.

Divested of their natural homes and hunting grounds, cut off from the renewable natural resources on which they depended, observing the continuing slaughter by visitors licensed to kill and construct, and disinherited from the financial or other benefits of these exercises, they became party to the most misguided and cynical game this century: the over-exploitation and destruction of the natural environment for the benefit of a few.

What is the point of only taking what you need and looking after your resources for the future, if they are simply going to be swiped by somebody else? Why not join in while the going is good and take the remaining few animals or trees whatever the cost, because you will never reinherit your traditional grounds.

So poaching and over-utilisation of the forests and conservation areas began in earnest. There is money to be made from ivory worth an average family's income for years at the risk of six months in gaol at no expense to you. Rhino horn as a homeopathic rheumatism cure is all the rage in the East (and some nearer to us here like to use it for adornment as dagger handles) and the cost of collecting this cure was infinitesimal compared to the poacher's gain – so the black and wide-lipped rhino are threatened.

Westerners have a bizarre trait of liking pets. Large numbers of tropical and exotic pets, together with tons of plants (orchids, cacti, and bulbs) are therefore forcibly removed from their natural environment and shipped daily from around the world to adorn the homes and egos of those with money. Most often the owners do not know how to care for these exotic pets, and care even less that tremendous suffering is involved. Six years ago we successfully brought about a European-wide ban on the bulk trade in tortoises where the UK alone was importing at the height of the trade 250,000 a year of which 80 per cent were dead within two years. The trade in birds (such as parrots), where animal welfare interests and conservation are similar, as in so many other cases, shows that in 1988 the UK imported 185,000 exotic specimens. 5,000 were dead on arrival and 21,000 in quarantine. How many more died in the exporting country or after the quarantine?

Even in Europe and many other countries in the so-called developed world, where sense and sensibility should abound, people pursue practices and habits which are destructive and expensive; which harm animals and plants – domestic, livestock and wildlife.

The complaints, cautions and convictions for offences relating to animals in the UK are horrifying, and are as much a reflection of the relative toughness of our laws as the number of predominantly domestic pets kept per capita. It is noteworthy that while complaints and cautions have increased since 1984 convictions have not. Is this perhaps a comment on the inadequacy of the law and the difficulty of policing and getting convictions?

Mention that a species is rare and the world wants it on its mantelpiece or in its collection. Today the locations of many rare or endangered species are closely guarded secrets. The Smithsonian in Washington will omit locations on their database for the sake of conservation and security. I and others hesitate even to mention that a particular species is rare in case it causes a demand to develop, even among our colleagues. Very rare species have been known to be eliminated precisely because they *are* rare and would, in the collector's opinion, be better off in a bottle in a museum for posterity.

Humans are also prone to excuse their habits by hi-jacking what they believe to be scientific objectivity and fact, or retrospectively to justify their ambitions by some gobbledygook about making a contribution to nature. Remove a fox from its territory and another will soon take its place – so where is fox-hunting's defence that it controls foxes? Circuses which use animals do so for profit, and there is no satisfactory scientific evidence that animals benefit in any way from their experiences in such an establishment – they cannot educate the public in the artificial environment of performing tricks, they only serve to entertain.

Zoos, botanical gardens and some circuses claim they are serving conservation by breeding animals or plants in captivity. But, until such establishments successfully re-establish wild populations which have become extinct or depleted in their natural homes, that claim is not entirely true. This requires massive investment in maintaining the habitat while the species is propagated in captivity and then a difficult and extensive period of re-introduction, re-stocking or translocation. Few projects have ever been successful. *But we need* zoos and botanical gardens to conserve species, because they are disappearing daily with dwindling habitats and pollution threatening the integrity of ecosystems, – *and* to educate the public, although there is no clear evidence that it *works*. Many species are having to be brought into captivity merely as an emergency measure because we cannot act fast enough, or effectively enough, in the wild and we do not know enough about most plants and animals to conserve them.

Zoos and botanical gardens the world over have to be conscious of their 'gate', the main source of income, and of course there is a temptation to become an entertainment rather than a serious zoo. To remove the fly-by-night and seasonal aquaria, and the bad zoos, the RSPCA was instrumental in bringing forward the Zoo Licensing Act which has dramatically improved the standard of zoos and the welfare of wild animals in captivity. We are lucky in this country that we have some of the better zoos, and indeed host what is widely recognised as the best, Jersey.

Captive propagation is one of the most important tools for the future of species. However, genetic changes occur in captive groups which can be counter-productive to conservation aims. Inbreeding depression can result when individuals which are too closely related reproduce and this diminishes survival of the young. In a study of 102 scimitar-horned oryx juvenile survival rates were shown to be inversely related to the degree of inbreeding. The breeding plan for this species is designed to minimise inbreeding. Moreover it is important to identify genetically suitable animals for reintroduction from zoos, where analysis can reveal which animals carry the under-represented founder oryx's genes and would therefore be good candidates. In maintaining captive breeding groups the aim must be to retain, if possible, the inbreeding coefficient of wild groups, and this is hampered not only by the limited captive stock available among the world's zoos but also our ignorance of the coefficient in the wild.

Recently the RSCPA helped to fund a behavioural enrichment study at Regent's Park which aims to improve the lot of captive animals by diminishing their stereotypical and aberrant behaviour patterns, and providing more stimulating and natural surroundings for the animals and a better educational experience for the public. When mealworms were given to a group of meerkats by means of a cleverly designed dispenser their activity increased enormously and the pattern was on a par with that of the wild populations; without such a dispenser they showed more lethargic, passive and atypical behaviour patterns.

I wish our widespread concern for captive animals and indeed plants extended to what is happening in the wild with the same intensity. Swans suffer from lead poisoning that comes from anglers' weights. After a scientific study the Society was instrumental in bringing about legislation (Control of Pollution (Anglers' Lead Weights) Regulations 1986 – effective 1 January 1987) prohibiting the importation and supply of lead weights for anglers. Recently we have learnt that the development of an effective, non-lead, 'green' shotgun cartridge is moving ahead.

In 1988 there was a seal epidemic when thousands of common seals died from phocine distemper virus. The RSPCA and Greenpeace did what they could to alleviate suffering and collected detailed scientific information. While the population now is holding its own, and antibodies are prevalent in all breeding adults, the mortality in the more polluted areas of the coast was significantly higher than elsewhere, provoking speculation that the pollution caused the epidemic. While the outbreak directed media attention to pollution in the North Sea, ascribing the guilt to pollution was premature. At least it has sparked off some serious research in determining whether organochlorides and PCBs, which do have an immunosuppressive effect and would make the seals vulnerable to viral attack, are the guilty parties.

Apart from the obvious welfare problems with snares, there is a wider perspective with regard to the number of badgers and other animals that get caught. During 1987 the Nature Conservancy Council reviewed Parts 1 and 2 of the Wildlife and Countryside Act 1981 and reported to the Department of the Environment. But this has not been published. However, a summary states: 'We also drew attention to problems such as ... deaths of significant numbers of protected mammals in snares used for rabbit and fox control.' In 1981, during the Committee stage of the Bill, the Under-Secretary of State for the Environment said: 'For the purposes of pest control, especially control of foxes and rabbits, there is no practical alternative to a snare well set by an experienced person and regularly inspected.'

In addition to the serious and much publicised problem of

badger baiting and digging, much of which occurs in my own county, and sett stopping, there is the appalling road-kill statistic of some 47,500 badgers a year. The RSPCA has produced a detailed manual to help Badger Groups, conservation officers and county trusts deal with problems and advise on road schemes. We have also backed scientific research into rehabilitation schemes and their effectiveness. We are concerned that rehabilitation may face the same problems as re-introduction or re-stocking in conservation – difficult, expensive, and the results often uncertain. However, there is no question that Wildlife Health centres are needed to improve our knowledge and ability to be effective in conserving and managing wildlife, and to improve its welfare.

So what is the way forward? How do we prevent this rapid slide into environmental devastation and the destruction of our wildlife? Because, have no doubt, it is *our* problem, since, to quote an old saying, 'If you aren't part of the solution you're part of the problem.'

Can we reduce population growth non-catastrophically? To date, that has been the only way – mass starvation, disease, AIDS, wars and insurrection, enforced transmigration and so on. Can we stabilise production where it is most needed, in the developing countries, or will their local political struggles always frustrate the establishment of a reliable and sustainable agricultural and natural resource-dependent plan?

Can we provide the means and technical expertise to help peoples avoid the need to destroy systems which may be their only lifeline? Can we develop simple and cheap alternatives to over-exploitation? In 1,402 sets of pelagic drift nets in the Pacific there were 208 fur seals, 914 dolphins, 22 turtles, 539 albatrosses, 8,536 shearwaters, 25 puffins and 17 storm petrels. Here, perhaps, green consumerism can try to get us to eat tuna that has been caught in a wildlife-friendly way! Gallup recently found that scientists are seen as responsible for environmental problems, although industrialists and politicians are regarded as even more responsible.

Can we avoid some of the worst aspects of the new game of the last decade of this century – the Green Game? The cynical exploitation of the latest political discovery, the environment – *because* there are real problems out there in Banbury, Bangladesh and Basutoland which can't wait, and they don't really care about our deliberating the issues and producing yet more paper, probably from their trees.

If we are to succeed we must have the best information possible from scientists, economists and other professionals. Which means more directed research to solve real problems; more scientific conservation, distinguishable from what has gone before; a better and more professional attitude towards animal welfare and conservation, and a greater willingness by academics and others to get involved professionally; a greater realisation by charities and other funders, even research councils, that research in conservation and welfare is vital and is often good, original research – without it no advances in society's legislation are possible.

We must embrace and involve the local peoples not just in Lusaka, or any capital city, but in Luangwa, in the countryside. The disenfranchised local people have a vested interest in their land and their animals and plants – something President Barco of Colombia recognised recently when he gave the Indians back their forests. We must allow and support the ethnic rights of local people to use their traditional resources, however distasteful it is to our urban and Western prejudices. If the local people are being manipulated by others for their gain then of course the situation is different. Many projects in Zimbabwe, Zambia, Indonesia and other places are now embracing the local people in the development of wildlife-oriented management programmes where they will, once again, be party to the decision-making and benefit from the activity. It is not reinventing the wheel, but adapting past methods to modern conditions and techniques, and reinvolving the true investors without whom conservation will not work – has not worked. Even in Europe it is necessary. For instance, until we did a NERC-funded project on tortoises in southern France the locals were not involved. Now, ten years later, the tortoise conservation project is self-funding, the toast of the local businessmen, embraced by the local people, forging ahead as one of the most influential conservation outfits in the area, exporting its expertise to other countries, and espoused by the local and national politicians. It is Franco-British co-operation at its best.

By manipulating the fungi which exist around the roots of all plants we can make the plant more efficient at taking up nutrients and make it grow quicker. This simple and inexpensive technique allows us to take the pressure off enlarged extended families with limited fields and enables them to grow more without fertilizers or more land. It also takes the pressure off the local forest or other local natural resources which do not have to be destroyed for short-term gains. It also helps us restore habitats quickly for conservation – for re-introduction programmes, for instance. We are trying to restore the deserts in the Middle East with indigenous species of plants by using another characteristic of mycorrhiza, namely the ability to make plants more drought-resistant and thus easier to establish. We have a few difficulties at the moment because the fungus does not impart resistance to wear, particularly from heavy armoured vehicles!

In Ujong Kulon, Indonesia, we are looking at novel microorganisms which might be useful to man. Indeed, they may provide an alternative to timber in justifying the economic sense of allowing forests to stay put, because without such a reason they will be chopped down. Countries, particularly developing countries, need the income, and unless the income is replaced by the international community they must seek the economic worth of their resources. Of course, where the wealth goes is a problem, since it often ends up in a few hands. We are also developing a technique which allows us to identify individuals, their sex and age, from dung, and this will be invaluable in conserving rare and secretive animals, such as the Javan rhino, using real data rather than the statistical guessing used at present.

Other strategies which recognise the new sense and the new possibilities are the wildlife/domestic stock village systems developing in Central Africa – systems not dissimilar to the self-sufficient, low-input philosophy that Gandhi was promoting before India became a monolithic Civil Service with centralised control which destroyed village integrity: the same problem that has caused thousands of Africans to return to their villages in the last twenty years, giving up their Government jobs for which they were never paid or even got their rations. Even in Europe we are setting aside whole farms for conservation because we don't need the food and it rationalises the subsidy system. But it causes rural unemployment unless some considerable thought is put into the change.

We must persuade industry not merely to give away their tax-deductable loot as a sop to worthy environmental causes and charities but actually to find ways of integrating environmental capital into their accounts, as part of their business – a kind of natural account – a problem we are researching at the moment.

We can make laws and regulations about pollution or wildlife trade until we are blue in the face, but without enough money for enforcement they will not be effective. In animal welfare and conservation the problem is international and immense. Banning importation, for example, often creates a market and demand for something else. We need to expunge the demand. It would be more effective to involve people by education, by making them part of the system so that they gain from helping, to give them a vested interest in maintaining the integrity of the ecosystem and the wildlife around them – very much cheaper than a law force, WWF and CITES secretariats. It works in Central America with green iguana which are no longer poached but protected by the people and the ex-poachers who are being trained to farm them.

It is clear that the issues of animal welfare and the environment are *the* issues of the late twentieth and the twenty-first centuries and that increasing knowledge and the application of appropriate methods together with the involvement of *all* the people will improve the plight of our beleaguered natural world.

3. Animal Protection and Environmentalism: The Background

James Serpell

Few people can fail to be impressed by the rate of growth of both the animal protection and environmental movements in the last twenty years, or by the extraordinary change in public attitudes with which this growth has been associated. But while this explosion of concern for the plight of animals, species and natural habitats may seem new and unprecedented, it is perhaps reassuring to discover that the basic issues involved belong to an ancient tradition.

In the majority of pre-agricultural, hunting and gathering societies, for example, respect for nature – in the broad sense – and respect for the feelings of individual animals are incorporated together into religious ideologies in the form of strict rules and prohibitions regarding the killing of animals and the exploitation of natural resources. Some of the central tenets of these belief systems are as follows:

1. Animals possess thoughts, feelings and social systems which are analogous, if not identical, to those of humans.
2. Animals (and, to a lesser extent, plants and natural phenomena) possess souls, spirits or essences which are effectively immortal and endowed with supernatural powers.
3. Animals willingly submit to being killed if they approve of the hunter or his actions.
4. The animal's essence (or the Spirits of Nature) will seek

redress or retribution against the hunter, his family or social group if it is killed without prior approval or proper conduct.

5. Retribution can take a variety of forms: members of the same species may become generally scarce; the hunter may have bad luck in future hunting, and/or he or a member of his family or social group may be afflicted with injury, illness, madness or even death.

Note the environmental connotations of the idea of game becoming scarce as the result of human misconduct; the notion that human transgressions can upset the overall balance of nature (see Nelson, 1986).

Because of these belief systems, subsistence hunters go to considerable lengths to win the animal's prior approval and avoid inciting its posthumous revenge. Typical examples of the kinds of ritual practices that are commonly observed include: (i) dietary and sexual abstinence before hunting, (ii) visionary experiences induced by drugs or fasting, (iii) ritual purification of hunter and weapons before hunting, (iv) offering of formal apology/excuse to the slain animal – blame-shifting, (v) offering of tokens of appeasement – food, tobacco, etc. – to the slain animal, (vi) ceremonial treatment of carcass – verbal flattery and solemnity, (vii) rules determining who may eat animals' flesh (which may include abstention by hunter and/or his entire kin group), (viii) avoidance of waste, (ix) avoidance of boasting, (x) ritual disposal of uneatable or unusable remains, and (xi) post-hunting purification of the hunter and/or his weapons (see e.g. Frazer, 1922; Hallowell, 1926; Benedict, 1929; Speck, 1977; Campbell, 1984; Serpell, 1986). Note again, the environmental implications of the idea of avoiding waste; never killing or exploiting natural resources in excess of one's needs (Nelson, 1986).

Thus, in their interactions with nature and with individual animals, traditional hunters face a difficult dilemma; a dilemma which is best expressed in their own words; for example, in the following statement by an Iglulik Eskimo:

> The greatest peril in life lies in the fact that human food consists entirely of souls. All the creatures that we have to kill and eat, all those that we have to strike down and destroy to make

> clothes for ourselves, have souls, like we have, souls that do not perish with the body, and which must therefore be propitiated lest they should avenge themselves on us for taking away their bodies (see Rasmussen, 1929).

Evidence from prehistoric ritual sites, such as the painted caves of western and central Europe, suggest that the same or similar traditions of behaviour towards animals and nature existed during the Palaeolithic some 20,000 years ago (Levine, 1971).

Anthropologists have spent the best part of a century debating the meaning and significance of these fascinating beliefs and rituals. Although no clear consensus has emerged from these discussions, one idea in particular has acquired a sizeable following. The theory, articulated formally by Malinowski (1954), states that these practices constitute a form of magical insurance policy against normal catastrophic events, such as accidents, sickness, hunting failure or famine. While they may not alter the actual risks that something will happen, they at least inspire the feeling that such events are not entirely outside the hunter's control. In other words, they make him feel less helpless in the face of adversity. Although not explicit in Malinowski's theory, it is apparent that hunter-gatherer belief systems also express a strong feeling of anxiety or guilt about killing and exploiting non-human-animals, hence the notion that punishment can only be avoided by behaving in a respectful way towards individual animals and nature in general. The hunter is thus motivated primarily by self-interest and pragmatism – the fear of possible retribution – even if he expresses these motives in religious and moral terms.

The Neolithic advent of farming about 10,000 years ago seems to have produced a fundamental shift in attitudes to animals and the natural world. According to the hunter-gatherer worldview, humans are bound by an elaborate mystical contract with the non-human world, and nature is seen as either neutral or benevolent as long as the terms of the contract – all the rules, rituals and prohibitions – are upheld. In post-Neolithic religious ideologies, however, attitudes to nature and to animal suffering became dissociated, and nature – in the sense of wilderness – came to be seen as fundamentally antagonistic to human interests; a source of weeds, pests, predators and the dark forces of chaos.

In all of the ancient agrarian civilisations, the original spirits of nature were depicted in increasingly ruthless, capricious and anthropomorphic terms. Eventually they acquired the status of gods and goddesses whose periodic tantrums brought epidemics, famines and other disasters raining down on the heads of long-suffering humanity. In classical Greece and Rome, wild nature was still regarded as a fearsome opponent, populated in folklore by an array of monstrous ogres, demons and other equally menacing supernatural beings. They included the forest god, Pan, who was believed to engender intense fear or 'panic' in those who were foolish enough to venture into remote and desolate places. Literary celebrations of nature at this time invariably referred to cultivated, pastoral landscapes (Serpell, 1986). Areas of true wilderness were maintained solely as hunting preserves for the ruling élite, whose sporting exploits were commonly used to illustrate their potency as rulers and conquerors (MacKenzie, 1989).

Once again this attitude to the natural environment was essentially pragmatic; farming involves replacing complex, natural biological communities with simplified, artificial systems dominated by only a handful of species. It is, by nature, expansionist because declining soil fertility on cultivated land necessitates a continual process of encroachment into previously undisturbed areas. Negative perceptions of wilderness helped to reinforce this process of agricultural expansion by, in effect, making a virtue out of necessity – by turning cultivation and agriculture into a form of semi-religious crusade (Thomas, 1983; Serpell, 1986).

Similar attitudes to the natural world persisted until very recently, and are still prevalent in many parts of the world, especially in rural areas. In northern Europe, however, factors such as population growth, urbanisation and industrialisation during the latter half of the nineteenth century produced a gradual change of heart, although the initial move towards the idea of protecting natural wilderness was encouraged primarily by European sportsmen who became concerned by the diminishing herds of game animals in the colonies (MacKenzie, 1989).

The modern environmental movement began to emerge during the post-war period, although its initial emphasis was still on protection rather than conservation, and most of the effort was directed towards preserving large animals and their habitats in the Third World. However, post-war industrialisation and the alarming rate of scientific and technological progress (particularly the discovery and use of atomic weapons) created a shift in public opinion that became increasingly evident during the 1950s and 60s, and culminated in the formation of various national and international groups dedicated to campaigning on behalf of the environment.

Rachel Carson's book *Silent Spring* which highlighted the dangers of industrial and agrochemical pollution back in 1962, was enormously influential, as were the writings of Paul Ehrlich in the early 1970s which helped to inspire the establishment of the Green movement. Doom-laden economic and environmental forecasts, such as *The Ecologist's Blueprint for Survival* (1970) and the Club of Rome's *Limits to Growth* (1972) also had an important impact by adding scientific credibility to the environmental debate. In spite of these developments, however, the rate of growth of the environmental movement in Europe remained fairly slow until 1986 when it suddenly accelerated, apparently in response to environmental disasters such as the explosion at the Chernobyl reactor in April of the same year. Since then, growth rates appear to have been exponential (see Figs 1-4).

Despite these apparently uniform trends throughout the movement, the environmental community is not entirely at one with itself. Many areas of disagreement over policy and philosophy exist both within and between organisations although, broadly speaking, opponents in the debate fall into two camps. One camp is occupied by the 'pragmatists' who emphasise conservation in association with human development and the sustainable use of natural resources – in effect, an exercise in damage limitation. This theme is clearly articulated in the IUCN's World Conservation Strategy (formulated in 1980). To quote from an IUCN brochure:

> Sustainable development – action that alters the environment so that it caters more effectively for human needs, without depleting renewable resources – is essential if the world is to be free from poverty and squalor ...

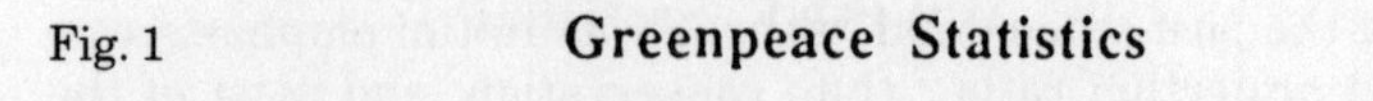

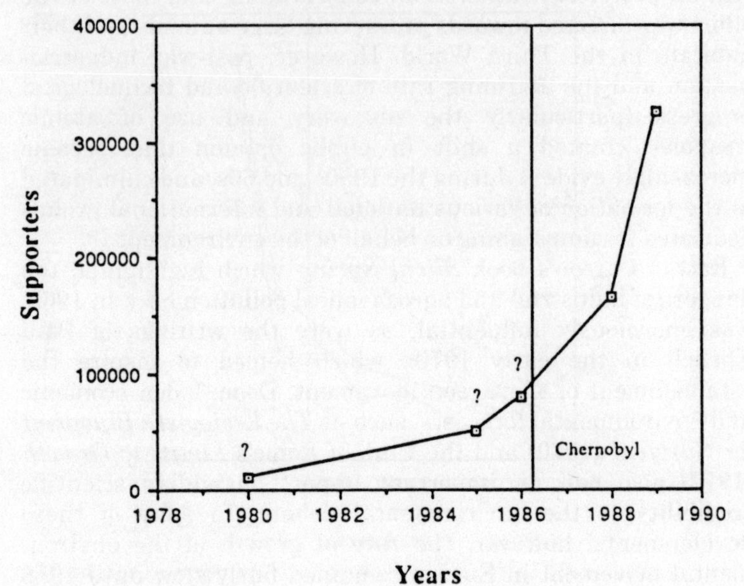

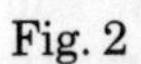

FoE Statistics

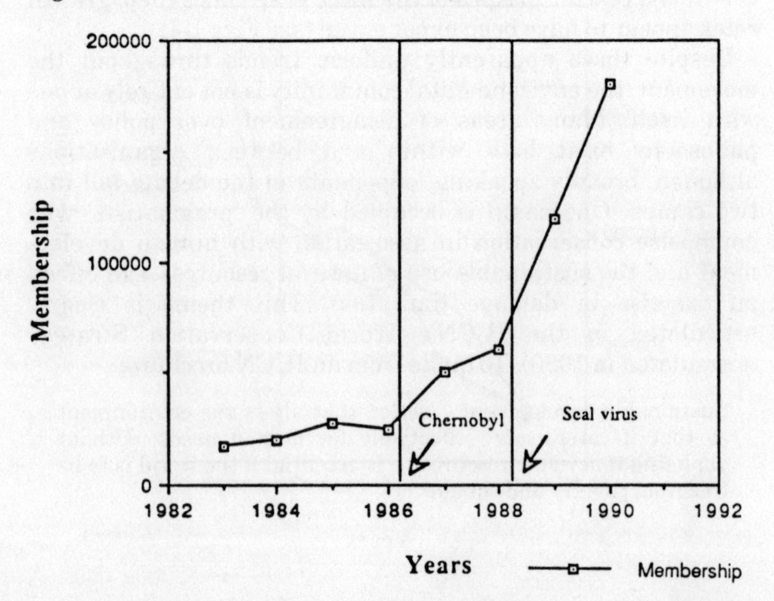

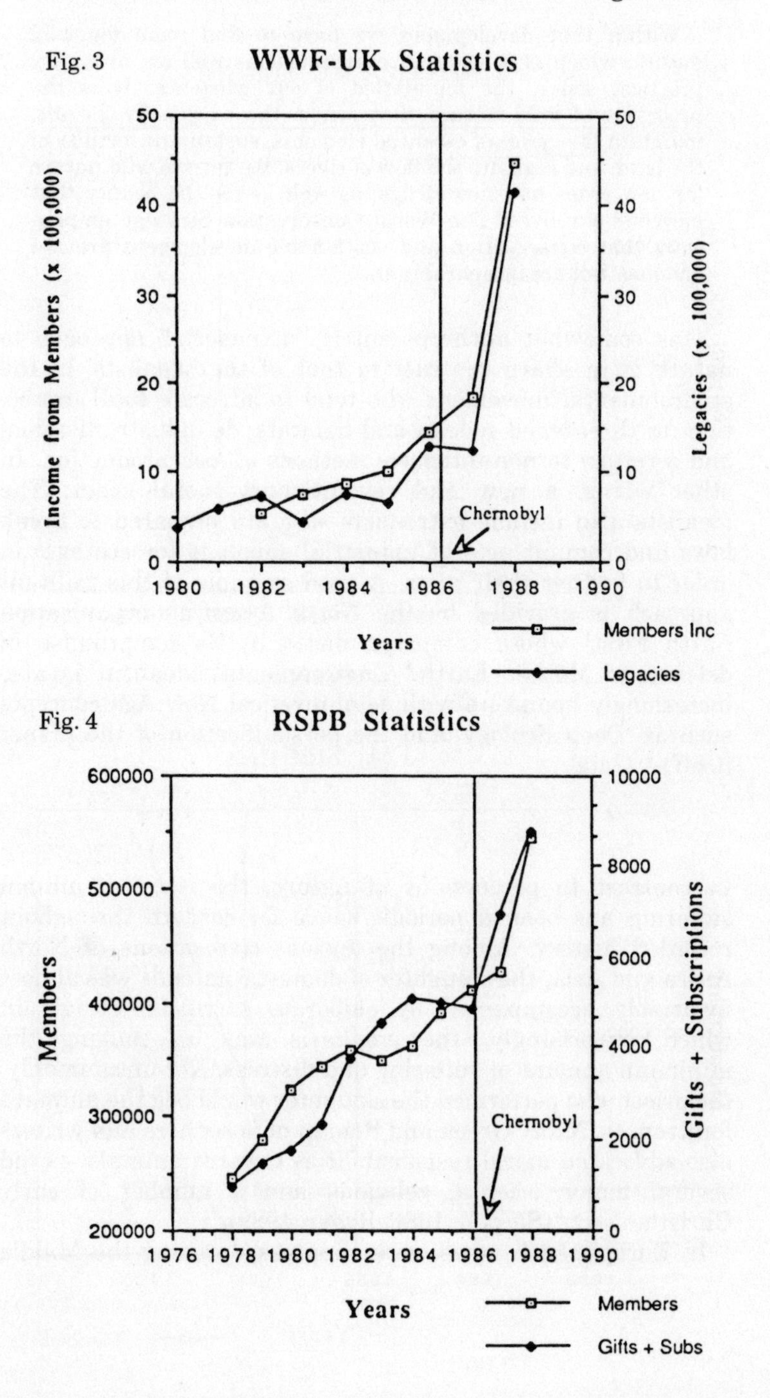
Fig. 3
WWF-UK Statistics
Income from Members (x 100,000)
Legacies (x 100,000)
50
40
30
20
10
0
1980
1982
1984
1986
1988
1990
Chernobyl
Years
Members Inc
Legacies
Fig. 4
RSPB Statistics
Members
Gifts + Subscriptions
600000
500000
400000
300000
200000
10000
8000
6000
4000
2000
0
1976
1978
1980
1982
1984
1986
1988
1990
Chernobyl
Years
Members
Gifts + Subs

> Within that development we have to find room for wild nature, which is a spiritual enrichment as well as, in a very practical sense, the foundation of our existence. It is the processes of wild nature that renew the oxygen in the air, maintain the cycles of essential elements, sustain the fertility of the land, and regulate the flow of rivers. We turn to wild nature for new crops and new drugs, as well as for the beauty that enriches our lives. The World Conservation Strategy emphasises that conservation and sustainable development are not enemies, but are inseparably one.

This somewhat anthropocentric, 'managerial' approach to nature is in sharp contrast to that of the 'idealists' in the environmental movement who tend to advocate total protection for threatened species and habitats, de-industrialisation, and a return to non-intensive methods of food production. In other words, a new and revolutionary moral order. The idealists also include extremists who are prepared to break laws and commit acts of industrial sabotage (or ecotage) in order to further their aims. A good example of this militant approach is provided by the North American organisation Earth First! whose campaign motto is 'No compromise in defense of Mother Earth.' Environmental idealism is also increasingly bound up with semi-mystical New Age concepts such as 'Deep Ecology' and the personification of the planet itself as 'Gaia'.

*

In contrast to perceptions of nature, the issue of animal suffering has been a periodic cause for concern throughout recorded history. Among the ancient civilisations of North Africa and Asia, the slaughter of domestic animals was almost invariably accompanied by elaborate sacrificial rituals in which, surprisingly, the emphasis was on causing the minimum amount of suffering and distress. Not uncommonly, the priest who performed the slaughter would beg the animal's forgiveness. Many Greek and Roman philosophers and writers also advocated moral responsibilities towards animals, as did several major oriental religions and a number of early Christian sects (Serpell, 1986, Ryder, 1989).

In Europe, such ideas were suppressed during the Middle

Ages and the Renaissance mainly in adherence to the views of St. Thomas Aquinas. According to the medieval interpretation of Genesis, animals were created by God purely to serve the interests of humans, and Aquinas argued from this that humans had no direct moral responsibilities towards animals at all. In his *Summa Theologiae* he proposed that:

> If in Holy Scripture there are found some injunctions forbidding the infliction of some cruelty towards brute animals ... this is either for removing a man's mind from exercising cruelty towards other men ... or because the injury inflicted on animals turns to a temporal loss for some man ...
>
> God's purpose in recommending kind treatment of brute creation is to dispose men to pity and tenderness towards one another.

The idea that humans had no direct moral responsibilities or duties to safeguard the welfare of animals was further reinforced in the seventeenth century by René Descartes' mechanistic proposition that only humans possessed rational souls and feelings, and that animals were essentially automata devoid of conscious sensation. Judging from the contents of a letter he wrote to a colleague, Descartes was well aware of the moral and practical implications of his theory. He wrote that it was 'not cruel to animals but, rather, indulgent to men ... since it absolves them of the suspicion of crime when they eat or kill animals'. Once again, an air of pragmatism pervades this statement. In a society where animals were being exploited with increasing intensity, self-justifying proposals of this kind allowed their suffering to be accepted with a clear conscience (Thomas, 1983).

Fortunately for animals, the views of this brilliant and eminent Frenchman were never popular in Britain, and it was in Britain towards the end of the eighteenth century that serious concerns about the welfare of animals eventually resurfaced. The leading light of this humane revival was Jeremy Bentham, whose *Introduction to the Principles of Morals and Legislation* contained the now famous statement to the effect that it was morally irrelevant whether animals were incapable of speech or conscious reasoning. The crucial question, according to Bentham, was: 'Can they suffer?' Ironically, the evidence provided by Cartesian vivisectors, who had already demonstrated the anatomical and physiological similarities between humans and non-humans, gave Bentham and his followers sufficient grounds for believing that animals could indeed experience pain and pleasure (Serpell, 1986; Ryder, 1989).

During the early part of the nineteenth century a spate of humane legislation was enacted and the SPCA (which later received royal patronage) was founded. Much of the early attention, however, was focused on curbing or banning the recreational pursuits of the working classes which included such activities as bull-baiting, badger-baiting, dog-fighting and cock-fighting. Middle- and upper-class sporting activities, such as fox-hunting and shooting, were effectively ignored (Ritvo, 1988). The anti-vivisection movement also emerged in England in the late nineteenth century but, again, it consisted mainly of middle- and upper-class pet-lovers, and much of their outrage was directed at foreign, rather than home-grown, scientists. In other words, the nineteenth century animal protection movement was largely class-oriented, and riddled with moral inconsistencies and complex ulterior motives.

Despite its early success and its many influential supporters and advocates, the animal protection movement was largely smothered by the onset of the First World War (Ryder, 1989). It appears that human preoccupations and concerns once again took precedence over the interests of non-human animals.

The recent revival of the movement began during the 1960s. According to Richard Ryder (1989) it was initiated by a division within the RSPCA over its persistent failure to oppose bloodsports. Ruth Harrison's attack on intensive farming practices in her book *Animal Machines* (1964) – with a foreword by Rachel Carson – was influential, as were the writings of Brigid Brophy and many others, including Ryder himself. The movement was given a further lift by the publication of Peter Singer's *Animal Liberation* (1975) – the first major philosophical discourse on the subject of animal rights – and this was soon followed by a number of other excellent works on the same theme. Now, like environmentalism, the animal protection movement appears to be split between pragmatic and idealistic factions. The former advocate continued animal use tempered by improvements in their welfare (a form of damage limitation), while the latter propose equal rights for animals and an end to their harmful exploitation (a new moral order). The idealistic arm of animal protectionism also includes its fair share of extremists, such as the now infamous Animal Liberation Front.

*

While it is convenient to categorise the divisions within the animal protection and environmental movements as either pragmatic or idealistic, it is important to remember that both are underpinned by, and financially dependent upon, a large reserve of grassroot supporters who, more often than not, have little knowledge or understanding of the complex practical and moral issues involved. How these people choose to allocate their support will ultimately determine the future of both movements.

Until very recently, supporters of animal protection or environmental causes appear to have been motivated primarily by feelings of empathy, sympathy or personal identification with animals, especially large, appealing and anthropomorphic animals. For this reason, environmental and conservation organisations have commonly resorted to using 'protectionist' images of animal suffering – slaughtered whales, poached and mutilated elephants, or endangered pandas – as fund-raising devices. Indeed, the Worldwide Fund for Nature has recently been criticised in the tabloid press for allegedly misleading its supporters for this reason. This traditional situation may now, however, be changing.

Recent incidents and events on the environmental stage – beginning, at least in Europe, with the explosion at the Chernobyl reactor – seem to have reawakened that ancient fear of nature's retribution that so haunted our hunting and gathering ancestors. Virtually every week we are warned in the media of further devastating environmental effects of our own past excesses; effects that threaten human as much as non-human life and livelihood. Judging from the trends illustrated in Figs. 1-4, environmental organisations have prospered greatly from this apparently self-interested shift in public opinion. But the lessons of history would suggest that the animal protection movement, with its emphasis on the welfare of individual animals, may experience some corresponding loss of support. More than anything else, however, the eventual outcome of such trends will depend on the rate and severity of environmental deterioration in future years.

If this deterioration continues or, indeed, accelerates, as the vast majority of scientists think it will, then the animal protection movement must surely join forces with the 'Greens' and, as far as possible, endorse their aims. For if the environmental movement fails in its objectives, we risk sinking into a post-industrial Dark Age in which human interests will, once again, eclipse those of other species. Already, at the grassroots level, the principles of 'deep ecology' and 'animal rights' appear to be merging and hybridising. But it remains to be seen whether this somewhat confused mixture of ideologies represents a realistic and coherent guiding force for the type of global change in human values that is so urgently needed at this time.

Acknowledgments

The author wishes to thank the Worldwide Fund for Nature (UK), Greenpeace (UK), Friends of the Earth, and the Royal Society for the Protection of Birds for kindly supplying statistics on their membership.

References

Benedict, R.F. 1929. The concept of the guardian spirit in North America. *Memoirs Amer. Anthropol. Assoc.* **29**, 3-93.

Campbell, J. 1984. *The Way of the Animal Powers*, Times Books, London.

Frazer, J.G. 1922. *The Golden Bough: a Study of Magic and Religion*, Macmillan, London.

Hallowell, A.I. 1926. Bear ceremonialism in the Northern Hemisphere. *American Anthropologist* **28** (1), 1-175.

Levine, M. 1981. Prehistoric art and ideology. In: *Man in Adaptation: the Institutional Framework.* ed. Y.A. Cohen, Aldine Press, Chicago, pp. 426-7.

MacKenzie, J.M. 1989. *The Empire of Nature: Hunting, Conservation and British Imperialism*, Manchester University Press, Manchester.

Malinowski, B. 1954. *Magic, Science and Religion*, Doubleday Anchor, Garden City, NY.

Nelson, R.K. 1986. A conservation ethic and environment: the Loyukon of Alaska. In: *Resource Managers: North American and Australian Hunter-gatherers*, ed. N.M. Williams & E.S. Hunn

(Institute of Aboriginal Studies, Canberra), pp. 21-8.
Rasmussen, K. 1929. Intellectual life of the Iglulik Eskimos. *Report of the Fifth Thule Expedition* 7 (1).
Ritvo, H. 1988. *The Animal Estate*, Harvard University Press, Cambridge, Mass.
Ryder, R.D. 1989. *Animal Revolution: Changing Attitudes Towards Speciesism*, Basil Blackwell, Oxford.
Serpell, J.A. 1986. *In the Company of Animals*, Blackwell, Oxford.
Singer, P. 1984. *Animal Liberation*, Thorson's, Wellingborough.
Speck, F.G. 1977. *Naskapi*, 3rd edition, University of Oklahoma Press, Norman.
Thomas, K. 1983. *Man and the Natural World: Changing Attitudes in England 1500-1800*, Allen Lane, London.

4. Animal Protection and Environmentalism: Science

Sidney Holt

I will begin by telling you that I now live on a farm close to a beautiful little town in Umbria, the region of St Francis. It is about the same size as Rye. We are happy that our streets are clean, that daily life is well-ordered, that our markets still sell locally home-produced produce and that we recycle our glass and our paper and our spent batteries. The self-employed mechanic who services my car – I am sometimes ashamed to say that I have a car – also sharpens sickles, sells strimmers and repairs motor cultivators. He is an active member of the World Wildlife Fund, completely untouched by Central Television's exposure a few weeks ago, and he carefully disposes of his old sump oil. In the surrounding countryside farming continues in a way that is very little different from what was left to us by the Romans, though sunflowers have recently begun to replace some of the olive trees. The feudal tenure system was only dismantled in the 1950s. And within the memory of my neighbours fields were ploughed by oxen. Now they use tractors, some pesticides, some inorganic fertilisers, but nevertheless most of the people of Umbria voted a few weeks ago in favour of a referendum which would have severely restricted the sale, and therefore the consumption, of pesticides. Still, at present we are lucky. Our well water is plentiful and drinkable. But I live in a transition society.

Most of my neighbours love children, and they are kind to animals, though they are not averse to eating their pet pigeons sometimes and wild pheasants. They don't talk much about the need to cull wild boar even though the boar do some damage. It is the hunters from the city who talk about that and also those who sell those hunters guns, ammunition and fancy uniforms. Nevertheless my neighbours like to eat salami with their olives and smoked ham with their figs, and so do most other Italians. Just up the hill from us is a small pig-raising factory which has just been built and, as the sun sets behind the hills of our old enemy Tuscany, across the valley, we can hear the squeals of feeding time and, we fear, of transport and slaughter time. We worry about the rotten lives of those pigs, which are among the most intelligent and sensitive of animals. We worry about the downhill movement of the slurry through our groundwater and into the pool at the bottom of the hill where the herons and frogs live. And we read that frogs are becoming very rare in Europe. And we wonder where all the feed for those pigs is coming from and what land devastation has been used to produce it. We are intensely conscious of the environmental and animal welfare issues in that one place.

In the Po Valley our future problems are multiplied more than a thousandfold. It is said that more pigs are reared there than there are people in the entire country. Italy now exports a lot of salami. The run-off from the pig factories is so high in nutrients and so voluminous that in warm summers the entire Adriatic stinks of rotting algae and dead fish. Summer resorts along the coast in the last two years have lost hundreds of millions of pounds in revenue.

Italy has an active and highly visible environmental movement. World Wildlife Fund Italia has broader interests than most WWF groups; it is more radical in its approach to problems. Greenpeace is newly established but expanding rapidly. An entirely homegrown product, the League for the Environment, is one of the most effective of all environmental groups in Europe. They have even launched a national daily newspaper. But they will all have to work hard together, and cleverly, if they are to save the Adriatic Sea and the coastal economy of the North East part of Italy.

Unfortunately the animal welfare movement in Italy is still weak and fragmented. Intensive indoor rearing of livestock is relatively new and people are only just beginning to realise what it means for the animals. It may be some time before the movement is strong enough to help the environmentalists in any significant way, both to save the Adriatic and to reinstitute sustainable and more human agriculture in the Po Valley. But I am convinced that lasting success in this will only come when both movements are strong.

Modern whaling was invented by Norwegians late in the nineteenth century. It involved using a cannon to fire a harpoon carrying an explosive grenade. Boats have since got more powerful. They now have equipment to make locating whales and chasing them more efficient, but otherwise the method has changed little in a hundred years. Concern about the inherent cruelty of this hardly appears in literature until after the Second World War. Efforts to control whaling between the wars was said to be for the purposes of resource conservation; that they were really concerned with managing the flow of whale oil through international markets.

Interestingly enough, concern both about resource conservation and cruelty was embodied in the immediate post-war years in one man, a Scotsman, Dr Harry Lillie. Lillie was the doctor on the British whaling factory, the *Southern Harvester*, in the Antarctic in 1946/47. According to the classic history of modern whaling by two Norwegian historians, Lillie 'had been so shocked by what the cruelty to whales involved that he tirelessly championed electric killing, which in his opinion would be more humane'. He persuaded the major animal protection societies, especially the University Federation for Animal Welfare, to campaign vigorously against the explosive grenade. I would say too that Lillie was a pioneer in using visual aids to get his point over, as Greenpeace and others now do so effectively with video cameras. He took his fairly primitive, but hardly portable, cine-camera and got, I am told, unique film of the whaling operations. I would like to trace that film, but I don't know where it is and where we could now see it.

Anyway, British companies undertook development studies to find a better method: that is, a more humane method. But they gave up when they failed to obtain financial assistance from the British government. According to the historians, the Norwegian companies also did experiments at about the same time. But their aims were clearly quite different from those of the British. The Norwegians were simply concerned 'with discovering more effective catching methods'. In 1956 Japanese companies experimented in the Antarctic with electrical equipment, but they found that the electric current impeded the blood circulation and this lowered the quality of the whale meat. Since the Japanese are interested in meat, not oil, as the Norwegians and British were then, that was a severe disadvantage and they abandoned their experiments.

Moving forward a little, in 1958 Lillie attended the first UN Conference on the Law of the Sea. He was an observer there for the World Federation for the Protection of Animals. He worked with others for a strong resolution against cruelty to marine animals, but with only modest success. The conference adopted a resolution which requested states 'to prescribe such methods for the catching of living creatures in the sea, particularly seal and whale, as to spare them as much suffering as possible'. Now I have been in this business for a long time, and I was at that conference, and I have to say that I had forgotten the resolution until I was reading things again in preparing for this talk. That resolution clearly withered on the vine.

Lillie next appears in the story addressing the 1965 meeting of the International Whaling Commission which had taken an intermittent and desultory interest in so-called humane killing of whales. The IWC is not required to work for more humane killing methods, but it can do so by virtue of the fact that it can recommend particular catching methods that are better than others. But Lillie's theme in 1965 was conservation, so he was working on both topics simultaneously. Apparently he got to hear about a particularly tricky deal prepared by three Japanese whaling companies to come with quota proposals, and he knew that one of the companies was taking a very different view from the other two, and he hoped that there could be a divide-and-rule situation set up. He found, for example, that one company was realising that the whaling situation had been allowed to become a terrible indictment of all those involved in the industry, the Governments concerned and the International Whaling Commission, but I am afraid to say that it was the attitudes of the other two companies that prevailed in Japan for the ensuing years.

In 1972 the United Nations called for a ten-year moratorium on all commercial whaling to be enacted through the IWC. The next ten years of international arguments about whaling are best known as the period in which many more countries joined or rejoined the IWC, when the Indian Ocean was designated as a whale sanctuary and when the sperm whale was effectively protected after 200 years of exploitation. But it was also the decade in which, successively year after year, proposals for a general moratorium were rejected by the Commission. That was finally adopted, as many people will know, in 1982. It was supposed to come into effect in 1985. In fact it came into effect only in 1988. So, during the period 1972 to 1979, the issue of humane killing practically disappeared from the IWC agenda. But in 1980 the IWC co-sponsored a meeting on cetacean behaviour and intelligence and the ethics of killing cetaceans. Although nothing became of this beyond an agreement that there were widely different views on the matter, that same year the Government of Australia proposed that the so called cull grenade should be banned.

I have to explain a little about this. The cull grenade is the old Norwegian method but without the explosive in the bomb; and the Spanish, Icelandic and Korean whalers had removed the explosive because the explosions were spoiling too much of the meat, which was a major export product to the Japanese market. Therefore the Australian move to make whaling more humane was in fact a move to get back to the way it had been after a serious deterioration. In fact the Minke whale, the smallest species, has always been hunted with a non-explosive grenade.

The role of Australia in all this is particularly important, as was its role in the successful campaign eventually to get a moratorium. Australia had been a whaling country until 1978 when an official enquiry, which was supported by all political parties, concluded that the public wished to see an end to whaling. Whaling in Australia was stopped. But the Australian Government went further and instructed its delegation to the IWC to work for a permanent global ban – not a moratorium, a ban – and at the same time to press for humane measures while any whaling continued. Then the bans on the cull grenade, released at the same time, came into effect for all species of whales. However, Norway and Japan, after the moratorium, continued so-called scientific whaling, which they were allowed to do by a little loophole slipped into the convention under which the IWC operates. They can still use, and have been using, cull grenades in the cause of science, even though they are banned for commercial purposes.

Iceland says that when it resumes commercial whaling, as it intends to do, it will withdraw its objections to the cull grenade ban. But Iceland and Norway have also said that if we don't let them start whaling next year, they will leave the International Whaling Commission. If they carried out their threat this would mean that neither the IWC's conservation measures nor the already weak and inhumane killing regulations would apply to them. But the success of the Australian move is quite important in a very concrete legal sense. We now here have, in the convention of the IWC, not only a possibility to enact regulations which would make whaling more humane, but the enactment of very specific regulations which establish a precedent that the Whaling Commission is formally involved in animal welfare issues. Of course, it is required not to challenge whaling in principle as such.

We also have a few little phrases in the UN's so-called Global Plan of Action for Marine Mammals which give us a small hook on which to hang international actions for the benefits of both whales and seals. One of the basic long-term objectives of the plan is to ensure that any exploitative use of a marine mammal population is conducted in a humane manner.

This year we successfully resisted enormous pressure from Iceland, Norway and Japan to lift the moratorium. But we do face a real possibility that some commercial whaling will be allowed to resume in 1992. So this is the time when some Governments are having to rethink their position and many non-governmental organisations to rethink their strategies. We have, as it were, gained time through talking about science and conservation. We will gain more time by trying to institute better policing, making improvements in the control of any future whaling. But ultimately we shall have to face the facts about whether or not whaling is acceptable to the peoples of the world or not. And of course the peoples of the world are intensely divided on the issue.

So our achievements are significant, but they are fragile, and I want to conclude by outlining what I think are the principal features of our work that have bought some success.

First, there has been a high degree of parallel and interactive effort by scientific, political and public information initiative over the last ten years. In public information I include Greenpeace-style actions, briefings to MPs, publications, briefings to the media, everything of that kind. At the same time, scientific research that is relevant has been supportive, and political lobbying through IWC delegations, primarily, and through their superiors in Government, has been intense and continuous.

The second feature of this modest success is that differences of opinion about tactics and ecology have, generally, been submerged in working towards clearly identified goals which have always been attached to a limited and defined time frame. Step by step. The strongest ecological difference is that between those who can accept whaling in principle so long as it is properly regulated and those who do not accept whaling in principle at all. And between these extremes there is a range of attitudes including the position of those who can accept whaling in principle if it can be made more humane in practice. But, of course, others insist that it could never be humane in practice because the essence of the cruelty is not only in causing a painful and prolonged death but, rather, in the harrowing chase of the animal, and moreover, of an animal which has not evolved with the typical biological characteristics of a prey species.

So where do we go from here? There are good reasons for continuing to support the moratorium. Greenpeace, the World Wildlife Fund and the International Fund for Animal Welfare are the three international organisations, the prime organisations, which have worked closely together for ten years, but with help from many local and national bodies. I think we are all agreed that we should aim at keeping the moratorium in place, at least until the year 2000 – I won't go into the reasons for that choice – and that meanwhile we don't necessarily have to try to resolve the ideological problems. If we can do that and if we can hold the dam, as it were, for a few more years, that will give us time to assemble the ethical arguments against whaling, and to get them diffused further in the world. Many people say generally that 'there should be no whaling for ethical reasons', but when you try to pin them down to a formulation of those ethics, you find it exceedingly difficult and, I am afraid to say, probably unconvincing to most people of the nations of the world.

So those are the kinds of things that exercise our minds now. There are many details. For example, we like the idea of benign scientific research, as we call it, to counter the whalers who say they will kill whales for science. On the other hand, the question has come up, should we support benign scientific research if its purposes are to find information that will simply make the management of future whaling more efficient? These are the sort of questions we face.

We also face demands for the culling of whales, as we face demands for the culling of seals and wild boar in Italy, because they eat things we want. Japan has an interesting theory about this. The Minke whales, which are numerous, should be culled because they are impeding the recovery of the endangered Blue Whale. The Icelanders and the Norwegians simply say, 'Let's kill the whales anyway because they are eating our fish'. There is not the slightest scientific evidence to support such arguments. But, at the same time, they are arguments which are extremely plausible to most people who don't think too deeply about it.

So one of the things we have learned – and the lesson must be carried forward – is that, even if scientists, scientific activities, political activities, legal activities and public awareness activities go ahead in concert, all the groups of people involved simply must learn to talk to one another. This has been a difficult thing to bring about. We are still not there. We don't think, if I may say so, that the philosophers are yet talking to us in a language that we understand, although some of us are beginning to grasp it. We have a lot to do in communications among ourselves and between the different disciplines and different complementary approaches. Moreover, the species involved, as everyone acknowledges, are rather special. They are special in international law, very special. We have, however, established the effectiveness of combined operations in science, politics and public information. We have established the multiplying effect of environmental and animal welfare organisations working together.

In the environmental movement the comparable issue is the rights of future generations of humans. That captures the essence of the long-term approach to environmental problems. Not just our rights but those of our descendants. Neither future generations nor the animals can speak for themselves or defend themselves. They have to be defended by proxy, and they are both in the same boat. If we can work together to achieve both sets of rights in the next ten years or so, we will have done, I think, a fantastic job.

We face what I call the conservationist fallacy in much of our debate between animal welfare people and environmentalists. Environmentalists as well as scientists have been afraid to admit to having emotions or sentiments. There has been too much diversion of activity towards the idea of maintaining simple diversity in the living systems of the planet. This can too easily move into saving endangered species and not caring for the Minke whales, the Harp seals, or the East African mammals. They are in their hundreds of thousands or millions. Animals have to be cared for because they are important in the world, not just because they are being driven to extinction. I get very impatient when I hear arguments about whether the whales are going to extinction, with the implication that, if you say 'no, they aren't', then to hell with them.

And the last lesson I think we have learnt is that we have to operate globally and internationally. We have to, for that is the nature of the world we are in. This is not to disparage local and national work – that's the basis of everything. But we can't solve our problems, and we certainly can't solve the problems of the whales, unless we work on the global scale.

5. Animal Rights: What's in a Name?

Tom Regan

Organised efforts to protect other animals are at an historic crossroads. Never before have so many joined in the struggle to bring significant improvements to their lives. Our numbers and shared values are making a difference in the political process, in the marketplace, in the classroom, even – on some occasions, thanks in large part to the indefatigable work of Andrew Linzey – in places of worship. Truly, we are a force to be reckoned with.

This reckoning sometimes takes bitter forms. Especially among those who make a living off the backs of other animals, whether this be in the name of science, commerce in flesh, or entertainment, for example, we are being 'reckoned with' with a vengeance. Steadily increasing amounts of their time, energy and money are being devoted to reckoning with us, not on the merits of the issues involved for the most part, but instead with a view to destroying our movement by discrediting those who comprise it. The old rhetoric of disdainful dismissal, the one that grouped all of us together as 'cranks', 'lunatics', 'freaks', or simple-minded members of an addled army of 'little old ladies in tennis shoes' – this old rhetoric is dead, or dying. In its place is a new rhetoric, an incendiary rhetoric, a rhetoric of vitriolic accusation. Today we are 'fanatics', 'extremists', or – the most frequently used verbal bomb, the one favoured even by the highest ranking public health official in the United States, Health and Human Services Secretary Louis Sullivan – 'terrorists'.

While it is important that we take stock of and combat the

fraudulent ways in which we are being described by those who oppose us, we should not be unmindful or insensitive to what we are saying about ourselves, of how *we* are describing who-we-are. For the plain fact is, we are saying many different things. We are against cruelty. We stand for animal welfare, for animal protection, for compassion, for human responsibility to the other animals. Our goal is animal liberation. We are part of a progressive social movement – the Animal Rights Movement. Are we all these things? Can we be?

In the remarks that follow I offer some answers to these questions, make some scattered observations about how these answers relate to concerns about the environment, and indicate where my own sympathies lie.

Why anti-cruelty is not enough

We do well to remember that societal opposition to cruelty to animals, especially opposition that has the force of law, is a comparatively recent development. In England we can date its beginning with the passage, on 22 June 1822, of the Ill-Treatment of Cattle Act, while in the United States we may point to the passage of anti-cruelty legislation by several of the states, beginning with New York in 1828. Sad to say, there are many countries in which no such laws exist, even to this day.

Laws without strong enforcement are words without deeds, and the tragic truth is that courts in both England and the United States have displayed a general unwillingness to mete out harsh punishment to those found guilty of cruelty to animals and an even greater reluctance to render guilty verdicts in the first place. In no small measure this is due to the concept of cruelty with which the judicial system has operated. Historically, to prohibit cruelty to animals has amounted to prohibiting the infliction of *unnecessary* pain, or *unjustified* pain, especially when the pain is *substantial* and the human agent has acted *wantonly* or *maliciously*, and *with intent*. A man who, for the sheer fun of it, intentionally torments and then sets fire to a cat, knowing full well what he is doing, is a paradigm example of what legal and moral opposition to cruelty to animals has meant historically.

Few there are who would speak in favour of cruelty to animals, as thus understood, and I take it that, whatever else our differences might be, at least we all agree that cruelty to other animals is morally vile, and morally vile for the same reasons as cruelty to human children, for example. Indeed I believe we can go further and state that this is a judgment in which the vast majority of British and American citizens agree.

But this consensus conceals important differences, especially those that concern *when* cruelty occurs. To be told that animals are treated cruelly when they are caused *unnecessary* or *unjustified* pain is of little use unless we are told *what counts* as unnecessary or unjustified pain. Not surprisingly, different people count differently.

A case in point is the use of the steel-jawed leghold trap by commercial trappers still common in the United States. For decades people have opposed the use of this trap on grounds of its cruelty, and among those who have done so many have called for the development and utilisation of what are called 'more humane methods' of trapping. For these people use of the steel-jawed leghold trap by commercial trappers is wrong because it causes too much pain, whereas other, 'more humane methods' of trapping would be permissible because the pain they cause, though real enough, is not excessive.

Stated in these simple terms, the anti-cruelty position's most obvious weakness is that it assumes that we already know that trapping wild animals is justified, if only it is done 'as humanely as possible'. However, since this very question – the question whether commercial trapping is morally justified – is open to serious debate, the anti-cruelty position, in its simple form, is question-begging at best, mistaken at worst.

This same observation can be applied to other ways in which we are describing ourselves. People who say they stand for animal protection, for compassion, for human responsibility towards the other animals, speak well and truly, as far as these descriptions go. The problem is, it often is not clear how far this is. If these descriptions assume that the only moral prohibition we must honour is the prohibition against cruelty, then they assume that it is *sometimes* morally permissible to cause animals pain, even substantial pain. Since whether this *is* permissible proves to be a widely disputed proposition, the position that animal protection, or compassion for animals, or our human responsibility to other animals are exhausted by the prohibition against cruelty also are question-begging at best, mistaken at worst.

In addition to these defects, there is another reason why merely being against cruelty to animals is not enough. In the end, all that the prohibition against cruelty forbids is that we unnecessarily or unjustifiably visit evil, in the form of pain, upon another animal. What this prohibition therefore fails to address or account for, is the obligation to *promote the good* of other animals. Perhaps no one sees this point better than St. Francis. Recall his observation: 'Not to hurt our humble brethren is our first duty to them, but to stop there is not enough. We have a higher mission – to be of service to them wherever they require it.'

The limits of animal welfare

If understood in a particular way, this Franciscan insight captures, I believe, the essence of those who stand for the promotion of animal welfare. To be for animal welfare, as distinct from merely being against animal cruelty, is to believe that we have a duty to improve the quality of animal life, by ensuring – so far as this is possible – that other animals are the beneficiaries of what is good for them, not merely that we should avoid being cruel to them.

The difference between these two views can be illustrated by considering the case of endangered species. Animal welfarists, because they are committed to promoting the good of these and other animals, seem to have an intelligible basis on which to rest their call for the preservation of natural habitat. After all, one does not promote the good of elephants and chimpanzees, for example, by destroying their natural homes. Those who limit animal protection to the prohibition against cruelty, by contrast, seem to have a less intelligible basis for preserving natural habitat. If they believe (as they often do) that human needs and interests are more important than the needs and interests of nonhuman animals, then they can – and, in fact, they often do – believe that we are justified in causing significant pain to animals, even if they belong to endangered species. Granting this much, these same peope can – and they often do – believe that the destruction of natural habitat is not wrong.

Though the two viewpoints differ in important ways, animal

welfarists, I believe, have the same strong public support as those who oppose cruelty to animals. I believe, that is, that most British and American people accept the proposition that we have a positive duty to help other animals when they are in need of it. Moreover, I believe that few people in this room will step forward to denounce the idea of animal welfare, as if it is a matter of indifference whether an animal's life is good or bad. There is, then, *something* in the idea of being for animal welfare we all can accept, just as there is *something* in the ideas of being against cruelty and for human responsibility and animal protection.

Nevertheless, as was true in the case of the anti-cruelty position, the pro-welfare stance is not free from serious problems. I shall comment on only one. Even if all informed people could agree concerning what animal welfare is, and how well various animals are faring – and these are large assumptions – the animal welfarist's position would remain controversial because of how it answers the question 'What may be done in the name of, or in pursuit of, animal welfare?' Historically, those who would describe themselves as 'animal welfarists' have answered this question in the following way.

'The welfare of nonhuman animals is important. But it is not the only thing that is important. Human interests and preferences also are important and, frequently, more important than the interests and preferences of other animals. For example, many people have a serious economic interest in the commercial exploitation of marine life; in addition, many others enjoy eating these animals. These people should be supportive of animal welfare, of course, but with the understanding that being in support of animal welfare is perfectly consistent with utilising animals for human preferences and interests.

'There is no question,' this view continues, 'that when animals in the sea are harvested we shorten their life. But – and this is an important "but" – ending the life of animals is not contrary to supporting animal welfare. If animals in the sea have fared well, all considered, up to the point when they are harvested, and if they are harvested humanely, then we do nothing wrong when we kill them.

'Morever, it is important to realise that a commitment to animal welfare is consistent with striving to improve the *overall* condition of those individuals who have a welfare, both humans and other animals, even if this means decreasing the welfare of some. Such circumstances often arise – in utilising nonhuman animals in biomedical research, for example, or in keeping members of endangered species in zoos. This is regrettable, certainly, and everything should be done to make the lives of these animals as good as practicable. In the end, however, to diminish the welfare of some animals is a price we must be willing to pay for making the world better for others, both human and nonhuman.'

I hope it is clear, from what I have said, that animal welfarists are people who attempt to serve two demanding moral masters. First, there is the demand that *individual animals* have a life that fares well, all considered. This is the demand that leads animal welfarists to call for improved living conditions for animals in laboratories or on the farm, for example. But, secondly, there is the demand that animal (including human) welfare be improved *in general*; and it is this demand that leads animal welfarists to permit the death of some animals, sometimes large numbers of them, and even to permit the agony of some, so that others might benefit.

When viewed in this light it should not be surprising that the loudest, most powerful voices being heard in the name of animal welfare – at least in the United States – are those who have a vested interest in the perpetuation of animal exploitation. By this I mean that those who identify themselves with the cause of animal welfare are increasingly those who speak for the commercial animal agriculture community, the bio-medical community, the hunting and trapping communities, and so on. In the United States, it is fair to say, these people have usurped the idea of animal welfare from the animal welfare societies that historically have helped police them.

And how can traditional advocates of animal welfare prove that these new champions of the welfare of animals must be mistaken? Will it be said that animals raised on close confinement systems, for example, do not fare well, all considered? Well, people who stake their opposition to factory-farming on this kind of consideration should be prepared for a long, heated debate, with one set of 'experts' declaring that thus-and-so is true, while another declares that it is not.

But even if the critics are right, and the quality of life for these animals can be improved, this will not change the system in any fundamental way. True, some more space might be provided; perhaps better ventilation; maybe a change in diet or exercise opportunities. The system of utilisation, that is, might be reformed, with a view to improving the welfare of the animals being utilised. Nevertheless the philosophy of animal welfare by its very nature permits utilising other animals for human purposes, even if this means (as it always does) that most of these animals will experience pain, frustration and other harms, and even if it means, as it almost always does, that these animals will have their life terminated prematurely. This is what I mean by saying that reforms within the system of utilisation will not change the system in any fundamental way.

Animal rights

Advocates of animal rights believe that more than reform of the system is needed. When a system is unjust to the core, abolition, not reform, is what respect for justice demands. There is, then, a fundamental moral difference between advocates of anti-cruelty, animal welfare and animal rights. Although the first two positions are committed to the view that we are *sometimes* justified in causing nonhuman animals significant pain, in pursuit of institutionalised human interests, animal rightists deny that we are ever justified in doing this. The true objective for which animal advocates should work, according to this view, is not to provide nonhuman animals with larger cages and stalls, but to empty them. If we describe ourselves as advocates of animal rights, therefore, it is quite different from saying that we rest our case with anti-cruelty or pro-welfare. We are abolitionists, not reformists.

In my view, for reasons I have set forth at length elsewhere, I believe that the philosophy of animal rights is the right philosophy. Am I right to adopt this stance? By my own lights, I think I am. The arguments for the abolitionist position are the best arguments, all considered. Or so I believe, and thus have I argued on numerous occasions in the past. You will be relieved to hear that I shall spare you the details of these arguments on this occasion. My interest here concerns how people who share my views should describe themselves. Not in terms of anti-cruelty. And not in terms of pro-welfare. I hope that is clear. But how, then?

Understanding 'animal liberation'

People who share my views can, and often do, describe themselves as being in favour of Animal Liberation. I believe this is an appropriate description. But I also believe it can be misunderstood.

One possible basis for Animal Liberation is an egalitarian interpretation of interests. On this view the interests of everyone affected by what we do must be taken into account, and equal interests must be counted equally. If only we would do this, we are to suppose, animals would be liberated.

This understanding of *liberation* is profoundly mistaken. To make this clearer, consider the case of human slavery. There is no question that the interests of slaves were often totally ignored, or that, when they were considered, they often were not counted equitably. This much granted, someone might maintain that the fundamental basis for the call to liberate slaves amounted to the dual demand that, first, their interests not be ignored, and, secondly, their interests be counted equitably.

This is not true. Merely to count the interests of slaves equitably is not equivalent to liberating them. Why? Because slaves can have their interests counted equitably *and still* remain in bondage. Why? Because there is no guarantee that, once their interests are counted equitably, they should be liberated (this will depend on adding up *all* the minuses, and *all* the pluses, for both slaves and those who profit from slavery).

Moreover – and more fundamentally – this way of thinking about Human Liberation has got things backwards. It is not that, in the face of a system of chattle slavery, we first insist on counting everyone's interests equitably and *then* see if slaves should be liberated; it is that we first recognise the moral imperative to liberate them, on grounds *other than* counting equal interests equally. Put another way, *after* human slaves have been liberated, *then* one might attempt to argue that a fair way to decide between competing social policies is to count everyone's interests and count equal interests equally. But it is mistaken to the point of being morally grotesque to argue that, *before* we can decide whether human slaves should be liberated, we first need to count everyone's interests, both slaves' and slave owners' alike, and count equal interests equally. The interests of those who profit from slavery should play no role whatsoever in deciding to abolish the institution from which they profit. The fact that the interests of slaves are not counted equitably by their oppressors proves to be a symptom, not the underlying reason, of the great evil human slaves are made to endure.

This great evil is rooted in systematic injustice. It is the right of slaves *to be free*, their right *not to be treated as another's property*, their right *not to be used as a mere means to another's end* – it is these basic moral *rights* that a system of chattle slavery systematically violates, not the principle that we must count equal interests equally. The very concept of *liberation* makes sense only if it is viewed against the backdrop of unjust oppression, and while the notion of unjust oppression no doubt assumes many guises, it is incomprehensible to me how we might understand it apart from the idea of the violation of basic moral rights.

There is, then, I believe, a much better way in which we can understand Animal Liberation than the way provided by an egalitarian interpretation of interests. It takes its cue from other kinds of liberation, and rests the call for Animal Liberation on the recognition of the rights of nonhuman animals, including in particular their right not to be treated as mere means to human ends. When viewed in this light, Animal Liberation is the goal for which the philosophy of animal rights is the philosophy. The two – Animal Liberation and Animal Rights – go together, like a hand in a glove.

Sources of resistance

Resistance to the philosophy of animal rights takes many forms, from the incredulous ('You can't be serious!') to the superficial ('What about carrots?'), and from the arrogant (as in the increasingly heard boast of American researchers, 'I'm a speciesist and proud of it!') to the deep. While most objections are to serious thinking what veneer is to seasoned wood, some

– I have in mind objections that some feminists bring against the idea of animal rights in particular and the notion of rights in general – deserve a serious hearing and patient exploration. I listen to, and patiently explore, the feminist challenge in a forthcoming book, and will again spare you an airing of my own views on this occasion. A second serious challenge, however, needs our attention here.

This challenge is the one emanating from environmentalists, especially so-called 'deep ecologists'. The fundamental focus of value, according to these thinkers, is the whole, not the part – the ecosystem, not the individuals who comprise it. A healthy ecosystem is one that is diverse, sustainable, and balanced; an unhealthy one is one that lacks one or another of these characteristics. Within a healthy ecosystem, individuals are expendable. Deer can be hunted, for example, whatever the reason, and nothing wrong is done *so long as* they are not overhunted. If that happens, then the ecosystem is thrown out of balance, diversity is diminished, and the community of life loses its sustainability. Sensitive wildlife management programmes, by contrast, developed on the basis of maximum sustainable yields – of seals or whales, deer or quail, or any species of wildlife, for that matter – promote the health of the overall life community.

Here, then, in the deep ecologist's environmental philosophy, the philosophy of animal rights finds a serious (and I dare say powerful) adversary. Notice, moreover, that this philosophy appears to be in harmony, at least in principle, with that of animal welfare and, adding certain plausible assumptions, anti-cruelty. The animal welfarist's position, like the deep ecologist's, is committed to permitting the sacrifice of some individuals for the greater good, and even the deep ecologists, notwithstanding their glorification of sport hunting (I have in mind such legendary figures as Aldo Leopold, Ortega y Gasset and the poet Gary Snyder), might agree that more humane forms of hunting and trapping are preferable to more barbaric ones. In the confrontation with deep ecology, it is the animal rights philosophy, not that of pro-welfare or anti-cruelty, that is the odd position out.

None of this is very surprising, actually. Despite their many differences, deep ecology, animal welfare, and anti-cruelty have some fundamental similarities, the most important of which is that individuals are morally expendable – expendable for the deep ecologist as long as the good of the biotic community is sustained or promoted, expendable for the animal welfarist as long as the welfare of others is protected or advanced, and expendable for those who accept the anti-cruelty position, as long as worthy ends are not obtained by means that cause excessive suffering.

Not so the philosophy of animal rights. This philosophy regards the individual's right to be treated with respect as inviolate. The rights of the individual are not to be violated in the name of some collective good, whether that good be the good of the ecosystem or the good of sentient life (both human and nonhuman), and independently of whether these rights are violated 'humanely' or otherwise. Thus, as I say, it is hardly surprising that, among those who wish to forge alliances with environmentalists, those who, like myself, work for the goal of animal liberation are likely to find the going rougher than those who are pro-welfare or anti-cruelty.

Even so, there are possible points of agreement – if not in principle, then at least in practice. The most obvious one is commercial animal agriculture in its dominant form. I mean factory-farming, of course. But I also have in mind the massive destruction of delicate, irreplaceable ecosystems (the rain forests of the world are the most obvious example), the massive pollution of the waters of the earth, the massive loss of top soil, the massive contribution to the greenhouse effect, and – lest we forget – the massive assault on human health that can be attributed directly and indirectly to the massive production and consumption of so-called 'food' animals that characterise our times. Unquestionably, this pattern of massive production and consumption is bad for the earth, bad for humans, and bad for the other animals. There is no serious argument against these findings. Only sophistry.

Here, then, we have the most obvious, the most important, opportunity for bridge-building, so obvious and important in fact that, in my view – and here I echo a judgment of Stephen Clark's which in times past I fiercely denied – an individual's or organisation's position on 'meat-eating', so-called, should be regarded as the decisive litmus test of their moral credibility. To the extent that individuals and organisations still support or tolerate meat consumption, to that extent they are part of the moral problem, not part of the moral solution.

By all means, then, I think bridges should be built between the environmental movement and the partisans of anti-cruelty, animal welfare, and animal rights. At the same time, however, I do not think that advocates of animal rights should be willing to sell their soul in order to build a bridge. If part of the deep ecologist's rationale for saving wilderness is so that future generations of humans can savour the orgiastic blood of the hunt (as Ortega y Gasset describes the recreational slaughter of wild animals), animal liberationists can and should unashamedly applaud the efforts to preserve, but not the reasons for doing so.

Aside from these sorts of problems, I believe all of us who presume to speak on behalf of the other animals should worry, not a little but a lot, about the possibility of the Goliath of contemporary environmental concerns co-opting the David of animal protection. Quite apart from questions of environmental impact, there is a distinctive animal-issue agenda we all can share and work on, whether we are pro-welfare, say, or animal rightists. Unless or until we codify this agenda and give it meaning through our cooperative efforts, those of us who care about what is happening to the other animals will remain individual, separate gears that do not mesh.

Here are some concrete examples of what I have in mind. The list that follows is hardly exhaustive. All of you will be able to add to it.

- The philosophy of animal rights calls for an end to the use of animals in cosmetic-testing in particular and product-testing in general.
- The philosophy of animal rights calls for an end to the coercive use of any animal in military research, or in such research topics as the deleterious effects of smoking, maternal deprivation and drug addiction.
- The philosophy of animal rights calls for an end to the traditions of 'sport' hunting and trapping of wildlife.
- The philosophy of animal rights calls for an end to the commerce in the skins of other animals for purposes of human vanity.
- The philosophy of animal rights calls for an end to the capture and training of wild animals, for purposes of entertainment.

Now, unless I am mistaken, those partisans of anti-cruelty or pro-welfare who are gathered here *also* accept these same aspirations. Partisans of these philososophies, in other words, as well as those who prefer to speak in the language of compassion or human responsibility or animal protection, share *some* of the same goals as animal rightists. Granted, the *reasons* each gives in support of these goals differ; and granted, there are *some* goals on the respective agendas of the competing philosophies that are not shared by the others. What is not to be granted is the pessimistic conviction that points of agreement cannot be found.

I conclude, then, not with stirring words of praise for the philosophy of animal rights, or with caustic words of censure for the other philosophies I have mentioned. Rather, I conclude by inviting all of us whose activism is shaped by our concern for what is happening to the other animals to make a renewed, conscientious, patient and determined effort to come together and forge a common agenda, even as we work, both as individuals and organisations, on projects that are uniquely our own. I call upon everyone to begin to work to create such an agenda in the coming months, mindful that each of us may have to make some compromises along the way if we are to end with something in which we all can believe. For the present, what is needed most is more cooperative work, and less competitive philosophising.

6. A Problem of Concern

Mary Midgley

I was glad to be given for this talk a problem question – animals and the environment. I take that to be a request for the difficulties and I am going to go in to those. My topic, I take it, is whether there is a necessary clash between concern for animals and concern for the environment as a whole. I am going to say that at the deep level there is not but at the ordinary, everyday level there often is and we need to take it quite seriously.

As most of us know, in the public perception these causes have often been seen as clashing. Twenty years ago when both these causes were beginning to gain wide support, many people saw them as clashing. There were some quite sharp interchanges which unfortunately are still there in the literature and I fear are not doing an awful lot of good. At that time deep ecologists tended to emphasise the value of the whole so exclusively that they seemed to rule out altogether any value for its parts and particularly for individuals, whether human or animal. On the other side, extreme animal liberationists for their part were occupied with extending the very demanding current conception of individual human rights to cover individual animals. And if you were to try to extend that very demanding conception over the dandelions and the tapeworms as well, you would be in trouble.

It sometimes seemed to me that animal rights must always prevail over every other claim, however strong, including claims from the environment. Each party tended to see its own central ideal and to look at the others concerned as a perverse distraction from it. Since that time I think that there has been great progress towards reconciliation and this has largely flowed from common sense and from a better understanding of the facts. As Tom Regan has pointed out, there is a convergence between these causes over a great deal of the range. People have begun to notice how much in practice the two converge. Animals and plants need each other.

The whole environment cannot be served except through its parts, and that has always meant that the ecological talk was unreal because one needed to say where should we start and you have to start somewhere.

Most threatened animals still live in the wild where their chances of surviving at all depend on their habitat. Equally the plants and rivers and so forth often need their accustomed animals. Obvious examples are pollinating creatures, insects, birds and bats, insectivorous creatures to keep the plant-destroying insects under control and creatures such as beavers in swamps which really are essential factors in the landscape.

On the other side, the ill-treatment of captive animals often has direct bad effects on the environment. Factory-farming makes pollution, excessive meat-eating upsets the ecological balance, trapping and hunting can injure habitat, and so on.

At the pragmatic level then, the rivalry has come to seem a lot less fierce than it did. The causes look less competitive and more convergent. The gradual perception of this has gone with the still more necessary shift by which people have at last gradually begun to realise that human welfare too converges very considerably with both these things. Tom Regan having said a bit about that, I will not say too much more. People have begun to notice that the biosphere is not just a theme park to take the children to on Saturday afternoon but a very necessary thing for human survival. No environment means no people, a dismal distorted environment means dismal distorted people. Slowly these are being seen gradually as not competitive but converging.

So there is some general practical convergence between all these causes, and in particular between those of animals and the environment. But, of course, we need rather more than that. We need to think out the principles involved. We would need to do this anyway because one ought to have one's ideas in some kind of order, even if the rough convergence that we have did not leave plenty of clashes remaining which, of course, it does.

But we need to get our moral thinking clear on this matter all the more because in the first stages of unbridled conflict both sides seem to be suggesting that there really was no moral problem at all because the principle that they were obsessed with was the only one that mattered. To each the other stand seemed an irrelevance: a perverse trivialisation, a distraction from what was obviously the only serious moral question arising. That kind of moral position can be described, I think quite rightly, as fanaticism. I am glad Tom Regan mentioned this word, because it is often used in the wrong sense, as he implied, simply for anyone whose ideals are rather extreme. What makes a fanatic is not having strong and extreme ideals oneself but taking no notice of other people's – not seeing the considerations that other people are concerned about.

And in order to get in to that state of mind one does not have to be a complete lifelong fanatic, one only has to be completely absorbed for the moment by a particular cause, and that kind of absorption is of course something which good causes often do seem to demand. All the same, nobody can afford to get stuck in that way of thinking. There is no single moral principle which is sole and supreme and can never conflict with any other. They can all conflict. So they have to be seen as part of a larger whole within which they can somehow be related. The impression that a simple one-sided morality is of itself nobler and more clear-headed than a complex one is false. We can always see this when we see somebody else doing it, but we have to do it ourselves as well. Any sane and workable approach to life obviously has to contain both an attitude to individuals and an attitude towards the whole. These cannot be in competition. They must be parts of a united attitude.

Unluckily our moral life is too complex for any single moral principle to be a despot over all the others. We are forced, somehow, to reconcile complementary principles and duties. This is hard enough in our own lives but it is doubly hard in public work where it calls on people devoted to different ideals to work together in mutual acceptance, and that means not just tolerating one another but respecting and understanding what the other is talking about. Now, it is not at all surprising that in the 70s both the deep ecologists and the animal liberationists were slow to see that need. Both causes were of the utmost importance. Both had been disgracefully neglected till then. Tunnel vision and mutual incomprehension were natural reactions. But since then there has been increasing realisation that the two causes must somehow be brought together. We are beginning to see that concern for the whole and concern for individuals are not alternatives, rivals between which we have to choose, but at a deep level belong together. The attempt to choose between them is an unreal project. Neither moral integrity nor logical consistency compels us to attempt it. The two concerns are complementary.

When they compete locally, they do so in the same way as other moral considerations which we know we have to reconcile somehow. This is nothing new. We are used to clashes between, for instance, justice and mercy on the human scene, between duties to those near us and to those further away, between all our duties to others and the claims of our own development and so forth. We know that in these cases we often do face a real choice of evils and we have to find some way of deciding which of these evils is the worst.

So, as far as general principles go, I think the issue between animals and the rest of the environment has become much easier in the last twenty years, and thank goodness for that. But there is still a lot of detailed work to do on genuine local clashes. There are plenty of these and we are not likely to get rid of them. I shall discuss only one type, but I think it is fairly widespread and will probably serve as an example: the kind that arises when a population of herbivores – deer, elephants, rabbits, monkeys – begins to damage its habitat seriously by overgrazing.

Now, most often of course, this begins to happen because of earlier human actions. People have encroached on the habitat, they have removed the predators or they have introduced the herbivores in the first place. But being aware of that guilt does not answer the question of what to do next. These past actions often cannot be undone; we have to think what we shall do. In cases where, after considering all alternatives, serious and disinterested ecologists and the like say that culling the herbivores seems to be the only practical cure, is that legitimate or ought we to ban all killing? Now I guess that is a real problem for those present. I want to say very generally that we have to avoid thinking about that sort of clash as an impossible dilemma, a blank, unintelligible conflict, a tribal row between unrelated moral principles each espoused by a separate group – a dispute that can only be settled by tribal warfare. Both the values involved here are surely recognisable to all of us. There is a real clash of evils. To leave a habitat to degenerate and perhaps be destroyed is to injure all its animals, including of course the species concerned. It may be to destroy them all and there are situations where that can happen. To legitimise culling is itself an evil, and it may risk encouraging other, much less justifiable, slaughter. There is a real difficulty. But some sort of compromise does have to be reached. I am going to point out the arguments for culling.

The central point I want to make is the general one, not just about culling: namely, that there really are arguments on both sides and we have to do justice to the complexity of the problem. In such hard cases, as also in the ones where either of these interests conflicts with the interests of humans, we need to proceed by careful study of all the local factors and not by general principles. And we must avoid dismissing a particular policy wholesale simply because the pretence of it has sometimes been used to justify iniquity. Culling is a good example here. It is the excuse given now for all hunting, but the misuse of a concept of a practice like that proves nothing about whether it is itself legitimate. The name of every decent practice gets used from time to time to justify something indecent. I am not talking about hunting being given the name of culling, I am talking about situations where culling does really look to be the only way to save the vegetation.

It seems to me of first importance to confront this kind of question realistically and not to discredit one's cause by refusing to admit that the clash exists. At a conference in San Francisco not so long ago, I encountered some people who want to deal with all these problems by contraception. They particularly recommend this for deer. Now just think for a minute what that involves. Contraceptives do not grow on trees in doses of which only one would be taken by each deer each year. To do that job you would have to take in all the deer in every year, weigh and measure them and give them their dose, and feed them while you did it. By the time you had let them out you would have domesticated deer who are no longer likely to be able to fend for and defend themselves as they previously did. You would have a lot of hinds who lived without having any fawns, and nobody quite knows what effect that would have. You have interfered in the situation in a way which may be – I don't necessarily say it is – very dangerous and you have to think out in detail how that is going to work. I have to say that they were also apparently making this suggestion for rats and mice. I did not hear them say this, but I am told that they do, and if you think what that would mean, I guess, whether you agree about the deer or not, that this is not a sensible suggestion. I am not saying that one might not come out with some new and splendid solution which was neither culling nor letting the environment go to pieces. I am very much in favour of doing that and I guess that since this conference has got the environment on its agenda we may hope to hear bright new suggestions of how to avoid dilemmas of that kind. What I am saying is not that culling is necessarily the right thing, but that these are genuine detailed practicable problems which must not be dismissed, as if they were easy, by solutions of the kind that I have just suggested. Anyway, these must not be dismissed with hasty suggestions; it is extremely important to my mind not to discredit the zoophile cause by sounding idiotic and to take great notice of the knowledgeable people who are concerned with managing these creatures even if one does not like their attitudes. One thing that struck me about this contraceptive suggestion was that it was being made by people who totally disapproved of all experimentation on animals. How would you get the contraceptives? I am sorry to be awkward, but I think you will see that these questions must be answered and if we are going to take extreme positions then we would have to do double the home work that the people do who don't want to.

In conclusion, I am sorry if what I have said seems to be one more version of 'on the one hand' and 'on the other'. I don't think I am taking this line merely because I have been corrupted by a philosophical training and cannot come off the fence. I think I am only saying that anyone who has followed the history of this controversy over the last twenty years will already see reason to think that the friction produced by quarrelling among good causes is enormous and it is a luxury that we simply cannot afford. None of us has a monopoly of moral insight and we have no choice but to work together somehow.

7. The Arrogance of Humanism*

Andrew Linzey

The SPCA was founded in 1824 by a little-known London clergyman, Arthur Broome. He called the first meeting together, served (unpaid) as the Society's first secretary, and ended up in prison paying for the Society's debts. Broome penned the 'First Prospectus of the SPCA' which spoke specifically of the need to extend Christian compassion to the whole world of 'animate beings'. The first minute-book declared that the Society was based specifically on the Christian faith and on Christian principles.

Contrast this example of Christian compassion with the recent debate of the General Synod of the Church of England meeting last July at York. A motion opposing cruelty and wanton killing and asking the Church Commissioners to 'critically review' hunting for sport and intensive farming on church-owned land *failed* overwhelmingly – 175 Synod members actually voted against discussing the motion at all.

How can we explain this ascendancy of Christian indifference over Christian compassion? One answer is that historically Christianity has shown precious little compassion for animals anyway. In the middle of the nineteenth century, for example, Pope Pius IX forbad the opening of an animal protection office in Rome on the grounds that humans had no duties to animals. Readers of my books will be only too aware of this negative tradition within Christianity which denies that animals have minds, reason, souls, sentience or status.

* A revised version of a Guest Editorial which appeared in *BBC Wildlife*, October 1990.

Pervasive though this negative tradition is, it doesn't quite answer why it is that in a *post-Christian* society there should continue to be so much indifference to the claims of animals. I suggest that it is humanism – both religious and secular – that is the dominant philosophical adversary. By 'humanism' I am not referring to people who don't believe in God. Nor do I mean people who are generally in favour of human happiness, welfare, dignity and rights, as indeed I am myself. I mean, rather, humanism defined as the 'religion of humanity', comprising that ancient notion that 'man is the *measure* of all things'. From this view it is a short step to 'man as the *master* of all things' too. Human interests become absolute. Animals are made – not for the glory of God – but for us.

The upshot of deifying humanity is this: animals are ours, animals are our property, animals are resources for us, animals are our tasters, animals are our tools. Animals are means to human ends. The prospect offered to us is clear: ever-increasing human management, dominance and control of the earth.

Some of us contemplate this prospect with horror. It occasions perhaps the greatest spiritual crisis in our world today. 'Man's fundamental desire,' wrote Jean Paul Sartre, 'is to be God.'

In one sense Christians have only themselves to blame. They have allowed their ancient texts, in particular the first chapter of Genesis, to be read in a way that supports, if not requires, human despotism. In fact the text suggests something quite different. Follow the sequence: humans are made in the image of God, given dominion, and then told to follow a vegetarian diet (Gen. 1:29). Herb-eating dominion is not despotism.

We need a conception of ourselves in the universe not as the master species but as the servant species: as the one being given responsibility for the whole and for the good of the whole. We must move from the idea that the animals were given to us and made for us, to the idea that we were made for creation, to serve it and ensure its continuance. This actually is little more than the theology of Genesis chapter two. The garden is made beautiful and abounds with life; humans are created specifically to 'take care of it' (Gen. 2:15).

According to Hazlitt, 'Man is the only species who can laugh or cry because he is the only being who knows the difference between what is and what should be'. This may be another example of the human species claiming too much for itself, but the moral point remains. We are the species now responsible for the global garden. With the power of technology we hold the earth in our hands.

Along with our new view of ourselves should go a new credo altogether. A fundamental part of it has to be this recognition: *animals have the right to be left alone*. Of course it is true that sometimes humans have to intervene in order to prevent the worst from happening – almost always the result of previous human intervention. But as a general principle the right of animals to be animals, to live in their space on God's good earth, is a moral principle I commend as a rule of thumb. 'Letting go' and 'letting be' should be the catchwords of this new credo.

In order to realise this new imperative we need three paradigm shifts in our thinking. The first concerns interrelationship. In the past we have thought of nature as simply 'out there' for our use. We are now beginning to realise that we are not just part of nature, we are inextricably related to nature. We must shift to realising that the destruction of nature is our destruction too.

The second concerns responsibility. Historically it goes without saying that we have used all kinds of nature, and especially animals, for human benefit. We hunt, ride, shoot, fish, eat, wear, trap, exhibit, factory-farm and experiment upon billions every year. We must shift from viewing animals as made for our benefit to thinking that we must be of benefit to them. We must move the debate about animals from how much harm we should inflict to the more fundamental issue of how much good we should do.

The third concerns cost. In the past animals have borne the cost of human 'progress' – whatever we conceive that to be. In the slaughter house, in the laboratory, in the factory farm, animals have paid the price of human wants. Now we must shift from thinking that human interests always come first to the idea that humans themselves should bear the cost of whatever progress there should be in the world today. I do not see the theological basis on which we can go on saying that the human species is of such overwhelming and unique and colossal significance that it justifies as a matter of course the institutional exploitation of billions of other species. In one sense, we are not worth it.

If this sounds a strange gospel coming from a theologian, let me say immediately that there is so much in the Bible about the awfulness, the cruelty and the unfaithfulness of human kind that we may be sometimes justified in wondering why God continues to love us at all. We do well to remember that, after all the violence that humans had created on the earth, God surveyed the debris and said 'he was sorry he made man' (Gen.6:7). It is a point of view for which now and then I have some sympathy.

I commend the Christian doctrine of costly service. None of us is pure as far as animal exploitation is concerned. We are all party to exploitation, whether through the food we eat, the products we buy, or the taxes we pay. Nevertheless we need to hold before ourselves the vision of the peaceable kingdom. We should want a world in which there will be no injury, no suffering, no wanton killing. To this end we all need to be engaged in a programme of progressive disengagement from injury to animals.

It is not enough to talk generally about reverence and respect any longer. We have to mean business, and this means taking on those people who, as a matter of business and commerce, profit from the exploitation of animals whether that exploitation takes place in the circus, the zoo, the slaughter-house, or the trade in exotic species or so-called 'food animals'. As consumers in a capitalist society we have great power to bring pressure to bear. If you had asked cosmetic companies ten years ago to stop experimenting on animals they would have replied, 'No alternative.' Now, thanks to hundreds, perhaps thousands of such requests, plus one or two boycotts, producers of cosmetics are learning the hard way that necessity is the mother of invention.

But it is not only to the institutionalised abuse of animals that we must turn if we are progressively to disengage ourselves. We have to examine our own personal lifestyle. In case there are any reading this who have still not seen the vision, allow me to spell it out in moral advice: If you attend zoos and circuses – find other entertainment; if you are engaged in intensive 'livestock' farming – throw away the systems of close confinement; if you are engaged in animal experimentation – find alternatives; and if you still eat meat – give it up.

Meat-eating in particular is morally indefensible. It may have been necessary for Jesus to have eaten a few fishes in order to survive in first-century Palestine, but it is not now necessary to feast on the bodies of dead animals in order to be healthy. We can have an adequate, even advantageous, diet without recourse to flesh. Taste is an insufficient moral basis for killing.

This moral challenge often comes hardest to those who think of themselves as environmentalists in particular. But it is difficult to see how we can have sensitivity to plants and rivers, trees and ecosystems if we have no sensitivity to the caged animal, or the animal undergoing product-testing or about to be slaughtered. I do not know what it means to talk about conservation while idling away one's leisure time in the killing of pheasants, foxes, deer and hares. True conservation and shooting (and hunting) for sport are a contradiction in terms.

Finally, let us rekindle that vision in Isaiah 11 where the lion does not eat the lamb but lies down in a symbiotic relationship with it. For those of you who judge this too visionary, let me remind you of the line from the Psalmist: 'Where there is no vision, *the people* perish.'

8. Animal Welfare and the Environment: Are they always Compatible?

David Wilkins

The title of this chapter poses the question whether a straightforward animal welfare approach is necessarily compatible with the concept of protecting our environment. I make no apologies for concentrating on issues which in environmental terms could be considered as being relatively minor compared with some of the major problems facing us today. In posing these questions I am not necessarily wanting to provide the answers, and it may be that there are no simple answers to some of these questions.

Protecting the environment means different things to different people, but in most cases it is the individual's own perception of what he or she wants from the environment. In other words it is a selfish conception and it is based on the individual's own experience. To some it will be an urban environment that they are looking to and within that concept will be the requirement for clean streets, no noise and fumes from traffic, no aircraft noise, access to local parks or open spaces, etc. To others it will be a rural environment which they are looking to protect. This might include a desire to see wild flowers and animals in a natural setting, possibly to see sheep and cattle grazing in fields, to have access to woodlands, country walks, to be able to climb hills and even mountains and to go down pot-holes.

While it is right, and of some urgency, to look at the global environment and to be involved in discussions regarding pollution of our oceans, the greenhouse effect, the destruction of rain forests in South America and so on, we should not lose sight of what is primarily the concern of the individual: that is, the local environment.

The RSPCA was founded on the concept of preventing cruelty, promoting kindness and alleviating suffering in animals. It follows, therefore, that our priorities are based on protecting the welfare not only of individual animals but of groups of animals, and this priority has to be followed even in circumstances where to carry out that protection might conceivably have an adverse effect on the environment.

In examining some of the questions posed, we have to accept that within the UK, and for that matter in most of the rest of the world, there is no such thing as a natural environment. The environment has been created as a result of natural evolution plus man's interference.

Man's ownership of animals has contributed to a great degree towards the creation of this semi-natural environment, at least within the world's land mass. It must follow, therefore, that the way man keeps animals contributes significantly to the environment and has a consequential effect on wild flora and fauna.

The husbandry of domesticated animals should ensure that their physiological and ethological needs are fulfilled. Two of the essential needs of animals are to have freedom of movement and to be able to perform most if not all natural behaviour patterns. Another is the company of other animals, particularly of like kind. These are important conditions for keeping both farm and companion animals.

In arguing that companion animals, particularly dogs and cats, require freedom of movement and the company of other animals, one has to accept that allowing cats to roam freely and dogs to have a period of exercise off the lead is necessary to ensure good animal welfare. However, the consequences of allowing cats to roam freely can be environmentally significant.

A study was carried out in a Bedfordshire village, i.e. a semi-rural environment, of predation by domestic cats over a one-year period and the results were published in a zoological journal in 1987. An assessment was made of the numbers and species of animals caught and killed by cats in and around this particular village. The quantity of animals killed was quite dramatic, and if one interpolates these figures into the nation as a whole one is talking about something like 70 million small mammals and birds killed by domestic cats every year. Some 20 million of these would be birds. It is argued, by many people, that this is an unacceptable price to pay for allowing our domestic cats to roam freely. On the other hand, could it also be argued that without this form of population control there might be an over-population of some wild species and that nature would have to find some other way of correcting it? From the cats' point of view, they were simply fulfilling their need for exercise and their natural hunting instinct. The alternative would be to keep cats indoors even though this would curtail some of their freedom of movement and all their natural hunting behaviour. However, many cats are already kept in this way in apartments and in most cases are apparently healthy and happy. Another consequence of keeping cats in this restricted way would be that you would prevent them from acting as predators of some anti-social species, e.g. rats and mice. Might it not follow that other steps would need to be taken to help curb local unacceptable populations of rats and mice? One could anticipate far more poisons being put down, and such activities must have a detrimental effect on the environment.

Companion animals provide a great benefit for a large number of people. There are some 7½ million dogs and 6½ million cats in the UK. It is important, therefore, to ask these questions even though the answers are not simple.

Although it is perceived by local authorities to be an environmental problem, dog-fouling is not necessarily harmful to the environment but of course is resented by humans for physical, visual, olfactory, health and aesthetic reasons. If one supports the view that dogs need a degree of freedom of movement, the opportunity to meet other dogs and to engage in natural behaviour, then this means that responsible owners would be justified in taking them to places where they can be let off the lead and allowed to run loose. While this may not be a problem in public parks and other open areas, it could be harmful to the environment if a dog were running loose in woodland, for example. Disturbance of nesting birds and all the other consequences of such free-roaming could reach significant proportions. A dog running loose which is not in the control of its owner can wreak havoc among sheep and cattle grazing in fields, particularly when two or more dogs come together and follow their natural pack-hunting instinct. Some breeds of dogs would be quite happy being exercised on a lead with the occasional contact with other dogs. However, such restrictive exercise would not satisfy the ethological requirements of breeds such as dalmatians, dobermanns and collies. Is the answer not to keep such breeds of dogs, or to accept that in doing so there is going to be a consequence of damage to the environment, albeit localised and perhaps, in terms of our global worries, extremely small?

The RSPCA advocates less intensive farming and, consequently, moves towards more extensive farming. Such farming practices will inevitably mean that more animals will be pastured out of doors, even though some of the livestock production methods could be described as semi-intensive. However, even the keeping of cattle, sheep, pigs and poultry in fields requires a degree of restraint in the form of fencing.

In an ideal world, such fencing would be entirely of natural hedgerows and ditches, but we know that it is inevitable that artificial fencing will provide the bulk of such restraint for cattle and for sheep. According to the Council for the Protection of Rural England, some 120,000 miles of hedgerow have been lost since 1947 and this accelerated during the 1980s and there is no evidence that this rate of loss has slowed down (in spite of the continued popularity of fox hunting). Barbed wire might well become more common than it is at the moment. Such fencing can interfere, as it does in many other parts of the world, with the natural movement of wildlife and can be directly responsible for injuries to animals like deer.

There are areas, such as the New Forest, Dartmoor and Exmoor, where ponies and sheep, and to a lesser extent cattle, are allowed to roam over a considerable amount of acreage in a relatively unrestricted way. In managing these open areas of moorland and forest there is often a conflict of interest between conservationists, environmentalists and those who wish to ensure the best conditions for the farm animals. Demands for more grass, less bracken, greater access to water are often objected to. A combination of lack of food and over-stocking can lead to poor conditions and sometimes death, particularly for the native ponies.

The question of hedgerows, maintaining natural areas of woodland, etc. leads me to look at another area which causes concern not just to the RSPCA but many other animal welfare groups. This is the question of field or blood sports. From an animal welfare point of view the chasing of a fox or a deer round the countryside with dogs and followed by men either on foot or mounted on horses is a cruel practice which cannot be justified. However, one of the arguments put forward by those who support all forms of field sports is that the landowners over whose land foxes and deer are being hunted and game birds shot, will maintain a more natural environment than if such activities did not take place. Even if there were some truth in such an argument it hardly justifies such an unacceptable form of activity.

It is relevant to note that the RSPB recently reported that some managers of grouse moors were deliberately killing one of Britain's rarest birds of prey – the Hen Harrier. Only 25 per cent of nests on managed grouse moors were successful compared with 75 per cent on unmanaged moors.

Ever since the RSPCA established a Working Party to look at the implications of fishing, we have been concerned about one of its conclusions, which is that fish should be given the benefit of the doubt with regard to their ability to experience pain. By no means has this matter been scientifically proved, but there is enough evidence to justify concern that fishing could cause pain to fish. The RSPCA's policy has been to recommend changes in many fishing practices in order to reduce the possibility of pain. We have also totally opposed some practices such as the use of live bait. It may be that, as more scientific information is gathered on fish physiology, the evidence for believing that fish feel pain might become overwhelming and the Society may have to come out firmly against this sport.

In defence of fishing it has been alleged that, were it not for fishermen on our rivers, accidental or deliberate pollution would not be detected so quickly. The fisherman on the bank could be the first person to notice that fish were dying or other water creatures were being affected by the pollutant that had suddenly appeared. Such a statement may be justified because the penalties imposed on industrial and agricultural concerns for discharging poisons into our rivers are still ridiculously low. The possibility of accidental or deliberate pollution of our rivers is always going to be present therefore, and unless some sophisticated measuring device is installed in all our rivers which can quickly detect pollution and hence lead to urgent action, this argument about allowing fishermen to continue to carry out their sport is quite a strong one from an environmental point of view.

On the other hand one must also accept that fishing has a harmful environmental effect: the contamination of our inland waters with discarded line and fishing hooks. Such debris from the practice of fishing leads to great suffering among wildlife and also among domesticated animals. Our Inspectorate have to attend regularly to cases of swans and other waterfowl entangled in line or swallowing hooks. It should also be remembered that, until legislation was introduced which prohibited the use of most lead fishing weights, the number of swans dying from lead poisoning had reached critical proportions.

This problem of lead poisoning in waterfowl is still present as lead is introduced into the environment in vast quantities each year by those who shoot, whether they are shooting birds or clay pigeons. Wildfowling can cause particular problems. It appears that cases of poisoning in the United Kingdom from this form of lead are as statistically significant as were those involving lead fishing weights, and in some parts of Europe there is increasing concern. In Denmark a study has revealed that 20 per cent of mallard ducks at post mortem had died of lead poisoning from lead shot pellets. In Holland about 400 tons of lead shot are scattered every year. 7 per cent of Bewick swans and 48 per cent of Whooper swans were found at post mortem to have died from lead shot poisoning.

I believe it is quite possible that within the next few years we might see European legislation which will not only follow that of the UK in prohibiting lead fishing weights but also outlaw the use of lead in cartridges.

The RSPCA concerns itself, as I have said before, with the individual as well as groups of animals. Never more so than in the case of those which are sick and injured, including wild animals. The Society has its own wildlife hospitals but there are many others in the UK, some run by individuals, some by organisations. The standards in many of them are excellent, but in others they can be low. However, that discussion will have to wait for another day.

The main point I want to make is that the only justification for treating the sick and injured wild animal is to be able eventually to restore it to its wild existence. But could it not be argued that the RSPCA, and others who carry out such a praiseworthy activity, are interfering with the natural selection process? In nature's terms it is the fittest that survive and therefore maintain the health of the population. Sickness and injury, from whatever cause, are frequently the natural method of eliminating the weak and maintaining genetic strength in a population.

As a veterinary surgeon I would never turn my back on a sick or injured animal. Nor would, or should, the RSPCA. Nevertheless I believe the question should be debated.

To end this chapter I would like to return to the question of livestock farming and take a further look at the balance that has to be drawn between animal welfare, conservation and protecting the environment.

It is regrettable that there is pressure on Europe's farmers to take agricultural land out of production, even to let it lie fallow. While there are problems if cattle and sheep are allowed to overgraze pasture, there would appear to be ample evidence to suggest that grazing cattle and sheep on natural grassland can be beneficial to maintaining an ecological balance. At the same time one must also recognise the importance of recreating other habitats such as wooded areas and ponds.

Grasslands provide more scope for combining conservation and good livestock husbandry. However, the growing number of vegetarians encourages the production of 'new' vegetable crops, and hence variety, while also reducing the demand for beef and lamb, and hence grass. It has been argued by a former Chief Advisory Officer of the Nature Conservancy Council that the implications for wildlife conservation may be considerable.

Getting the balance right is always going to be difficult, but it should not be impossible.

In our efforts to promote extensification of livestock production, it is right that we should question whether livestock production should be allowed unrestricted use of technology in order to produce maximum output from the minimum amount of land. In Europe there are already signs that more and more people are taking this matter seriously, hence the EC ban on hormones for growth promotion and the opposition to BST.

Extensive farming will also mean that some of the land will have to be farmed at below-optimum intensity leading to consequent lower profitability. Farmers will need to receive financial compensation to operate many extensive livestock production systems. We must recognise that it will have to be the consumer who pays, and it is up to animal welfare organisations such as the RSPCA to ensure that the increased price for food will be seen to be acceptable because of an improvement both in animal welfare and environmental protection.

Finally, we must not ignore the fact that research and careful planning is needed in order to devise extensive husbandry systems that are humane, commercially feasible and protective of the environment. I am quite certain that this can be achieved. It will be decades before most countries outside Western Europe allow themselves the luxury of being nice to animals, but the earlier we lay the technical foundation the earlier that day may come.

9. Husbandry Regained: Animals in Sustainable Agriculture

John Webster

It was easy, when we were predominantly discussing philosophy, to link farm animal welfare and protection of the environment, in so far as they are both concerned with what qualifies us to consider ourselves to be good people. Today, we are dealing with what I unashamedly and unapologetically call Utilitarian – the strictly pragmatic link, or otherwise, between these two elements. It is too simple just to link the protection of the environment and the protection of animals, as it is equally simple to impose blanket condemnation on modern intensive agriculture, especially on the factory-farming of animals. It is perfectly true that modern factory-farming can sometimes be accused of engendering cruelty, waste, pollution and unsafe foods. But blanket condemnation, or the overall linking of good things like the environment and animal welfare, does lay us open to the charge of thinking in a way that is, at best, wishful and, at worst, woolly. I must, therefore, introduce some rather harsh facts of life which we may choose to ignore but from which we cannot escape.

The title of this chapter is an optimistic one. But before proceeding to optimism I have to introduce some harsh truths. The first is that nature itelf is an omnivore. All life-forms exist ultimately to be eaten or otherwise consumed by animals: by predators, for example, (you can include man), by microbes or by auto-digestion. Our huggable bunny may well be eaten by a fox, it may well be eaten by us, or it may start to be eaten by micro-organisms, die and be finished off by other micro-organisms. The same more or less applies to us. We probably escape those first fates rather more than the rabbit. But we have a greater probability that we shall self-destruct. The malignant cells in our bodies will start the process of digesting us before we die and then the micro-organisms can take over later. This all looks very tidy, and everything is recycled. It ensures that life goes on. The death of the individual is essential to the survival of the biosphere. Now individual humans may honourably choose not to kill and or eat certain species of animals. This is a perfectly honourable aim but it does not escape the issue. It does not protect the animal from consumption and death. It merely adjusts the methods.

The second thing we cannot escape is that man has dominion over the animals, whether we like it or not. I think it was Bertrand Russell who said that 'all species have inclinations towards totalitarianism'. That is to say, all species have tried to convert the whole world in to themselves if they possibly can. The fact is that we are rather more successful at it than other species. Wherever the earth will support life for man, it is man who decides the nature, the extent and the policy of the habitat and life for other species. Now we may be baddies and decide to erect a battery-house for laying hens, or we may be goodies and decide to create a wilderness park for wildlife. But in each case the decision has been ours, not theirs.

The third point you are going to like better. That is that industrialised agriculture in its current form is neither sustainable nor exportable to the Third World. There are a number of reasons for this which could take all day to expound, but the main reason and the one I shall elaborate is that industrialised agriculture nearly always consumes more energy than it produces and is living off capital in the form of fossil fuels. This capital is running out, and if we export industrial agriculture to the Third World it will run out faster.

Let us examine the evolution of animal husbandry in the light of these three great, if harsh, truths. In the beginning, as man developed agriculture and agriculture begat civilisation, animals were economically and ecologically essential parts of the overall enterprise. Sheep and goats grazed the plains, the common land, as they do now in Africa. This was inefficient, it seems, according to modern animal scientists, but they were corralled at night and brought fertiliser home to the cultivated land around the farmstead. In that it was very efficient. Pigs and poultry scavenged for food around the farm. All this minimised waste and thus ensured that each party contributed its fair share to the society. In a sentence: for six months the farmer fed the pig, and for the next six months the pig fed the farmer, which is fair. The system was sustainable, without need for ethics. Men cared for animals in proportion to their value. And man, lacking such things as machinery, petroleum, pesticides, etc, did not greatly disturb the environment. Man was not more ethical then. He was simply less powerful and, therefore, less dangerous. But it was a sustainable, though not very efficient, society.

The industrialisation of animal production has been a phenomenon of the last fifty years, which is not very long in recorded history. Its rise can be attributed mainly to increased productivity of cereals and grasses from increased mechanisation and fertilisers, both of which depend on fossil fuel, therefore using capital to grow more cereals and grasses. This has created more food for everybody and, therefore, created more food that is available to feed animals.

The second thing is largely due to the veterinary profession: the control of infectious disease by vaccination and by antibiotics. This has made it possible to keep much greater numbers of animals in much greater stocking densities in intensive housing, and it is this that has made factory-farming possible.

The final point is that internationally increasing wealth has increased the demand for animal produce. Generally speaking, as one proceeds from total poverty throughout the world over most of recorded history, increasing wealth has increased demand for animal produce.

Let us digress slightly to talk about efficiency in agriculture, comparing fairly modern production of wheat, which is a very efficient crop in the USA, with production of wheat from bullock-power in India. The first thing to say is that this is one of those things that can disappoint us. Bullock power to produce wheat is very inefficient. Not only does it not produce much wheat, as we well know, but, in fact, it is not creating as much energy output as energy input going in to the system. It only works, in fact, partly because people do not eat very much and partly because most of the work, the energy needed to fire the bullock, is not coming from wheat, it is coming from food that is not directly available to man. Mechanisation of the USA has got wheat production to 44 per cent more output than input, but a substantial amount of this is fossil fuel and that is at the farm gate. By the time we get it spread, we only have a 10 per cent gain in terms of the total energetics of the system, and if you put in fossil fuel for machinery and for fertilisers we are running at a loss.

I am going to criticise modern farming methods, I promise you, but before I do it is also worth remembering that the primary beneficiary has been the consumer. Food is cheaper in real terms, I think we have also agreed. What we do not tend to agree about, and what I should reassure you about, is that food is also safer than it was. I am not going to go in to all the details, but I give you one example. BSE is creating panic to a certain extent, but BTB used to kill an awful lot of children. At the beginning of the 1920s TB of bovine origin from cattle was killing over 3,000 people a year in the United Kingdom. This is a pretty staggering statistic which we should remember when we are considering the relative risk, then and now. There is a risk in eating animal produce, there has always been a risk in eating animal produce, but it is not statistically getting worse.

My main criticism of intensive agricultural production, and of animal farming in particular, is that it has been locked for too long into a model-T-Ford-type philosophy, geared to produce a standard commodity as cheaply as possible. This narrow thinking combined with a short-term expediency of the free market has, in fact, driven farmers into an unsustainable position by over-consumption of resources, by pollution and by standards of animal care that are increasingly out of touch with consumer demand. Criticisms of factory farming have been rehearsed often enough. I do not intend to go through them here. What I hope to do from now on is to offer constructive suggestions as to how we might go forward.

Having, in our society, achieved a quantity of food to meet our needs, we can now afford to seek more quality. Ideally, this implies food that is wholesome, tasty and safe, from husbandry systems that abuse neither farm animals nor the environment. However, we have to decide for ourselves. It is our decision, how much quality we can afford. Starving people in the sub-Sahara cannot afford much quality, though it is fair to say that their problems are more political than strictly agricultural. Closer to home we have to decide whether, for example, to recognise that an increase in food prices imposed as a result of welfare standards demanded by the middle classes would be rather like the poll tax. It would impose an unfair burden on the poor.

Another thing we have to consider is that we cannot afford to dispense with farm animals altogether. And this is the point made by David Wilkins. It is absolutely true that many forms of modern, intensive livestock production are extremely inefficient. Here we are looking at the same argument using the energy input in absolute terms. Meat production is obviously inefficient for all sorts of reasons and meat production from beef reared intensively is really wasteful by all sorts of criteria; it is very expensive on fossil fuel, it is not very productive in terms of food energy and the animals are obviously having to be killed in the process. But the use of range cattle, though the yield is lower and we are talking now about extensification, is sustainable, largely because it can be sustained with minimal input from fossil fuel. Extensification for meat production purposes is therefore an option that is consistent with sustainable agriculture.

The other thing one can do is once again increasingly to use food that we, ourselves, cannot or will not use, and the imposition of quotas which has put a degree of extensification on dairy production, has in fact encouraged this trend.

Consider some simple examples from the University Farm at Bristol of how we fed our cows before and after the imposition of quotas. We have a pretty typical farm. Before quotas, about 50 per cent of the food energy going in to our dairy cows was in the form of cereals: food that could be directly used by man, because in those days it was cost-effective to get as much milk as possible out of individual cows. That gave one the best financial returns. Now, when the output is fixed, there are far greater incentives to go for lower cost inputs. That is the pathway we have gone down, and in consequence we have reduced the amount of food that is given to our cows that could be eaten by man from 50 per cent to 14 per cent by getting the input from grass and porridge oats: food that would otherwise be wasted in a system that is not using these animals to pick it up on the way. I would say, incidentally, without elaborating, that this is potentially beneficial to the health of the cows, because we do know that the major problems of ill health in cows are the production diseases associated with very high yields.

We can't dispense with animals altogether. Another suggestion one tends to hear is that animals should live on our farms but not be killed, only providing us with milk, wool and manure. Now this state is approachable in the extreme pastoral communities – the Indians with their bullocks – but it is not very efficient. It is also approachable at the other end of the spectrum, which is filled by the middle-class peasant or designer-green who has a few pet animals to fit in with a rural lifestyle. In this case the animals get quite a good deal, but in neither case do they contribute much to wealth. As a general rule, whatever we may like to think, the less wealth generated by an animal as an individual the less attention is paid to its welfare, such as Merino sheep in Australia and Angora goats in South Africa existing only to produce wool; the individual battery hen in Britain, too, has very little cash value, and therefore very little attention is paid to her welfare. The implication of this is that well-meaning attempts to avoid killing animals, can, in fact, be injurious to their health. We cannot wash our hands of this.

Environmental pressures give us no option but to exploit animals. Having accepted that, we then have the obligation to recognise them not as mere units of production but as beings with rights to a reasonable quality of life and a gentle death. The quality of life that we can afford to give them will depend, whether we like it or not, on the value of their contribution to us. I have defined quality of life for farm animals, or welfare for farm animals elsewhere.

We need to know something of an animal's mind. If we observe, for example, a sow confined to a stall we cannot simply conclude that she is distressed without asking her rather more subtle questions. For example, how does the quality of her environment, as she perceives it, now come up to her initial expectations? And has it got better or worse? These may in fact sound like rather subtle questions to ask a pig, but they are well within the scope of modern animal psychology. Indeed, as experimental psychology of animals evolves from simple behaviourism – the simple response experiments of Skinner – to the more complex information-theory of positive science, it becomes ever clearer that the minds of animals – and I use the word advisedly, meaning their capacity to reason from stored information – are extremely complex, and this imposes a greater responsibility on us. It is just that, until recently, we never thought, or did not know how, to ask. Now, as we learn to ask animals the right questions, we can avoid doing more harm than good through well-meaning concepts of what constitutes a happy life. For example, if we were to enforce so-called free-range systems for laying hens that increased the incidence of death, infectious disease, aggression, pain and fear, it might make us feel fairly good, but it would not do a lot of good for the hens. There are various ways of improving the lot of hens but we do need to ask the hens themselves rather than make up their minds for them.

There is little doubt now that we can go forward. We are beginning to look in the right direction, and there is a genuine urgency. The very fact that we are considering aspects of animal welfare suggests that we are now heading in the right direction. These are the sort of avenues by which we should approach proper research as to the quality of the environment as perceived by the animal, proper use of education to disseminate that knowledge and minimal legislation where necessary. There is no doubt whatsoever that the European Community will improve minimum standards for farm animals by legislation. Inevitably, there is less agreement as to what these standards should be. I have argued before, and shall again, that the farming industry has nothing to fear from such legislation so long as it is fairly enforced. And indeed it would help restore pride in animal husbandry without bankrupting farmers in the process.

One effect of this legislation will be to stimulate some degree of intensification. This should be environmentally friendly. Some of the main diseases of intensification – metabolic disorders in dairy cows, bone disorders in poultry – could be reduced. This is good for welfare. However, the costs of production will increase as farmers are made to invest more time and money in each animal, and these costs must be met by the consumer. However, the effects of legislation will, inevitably, be small relative to the impact of economic sources which we cannot ignore. And these will themselves be determined by developments in such things as personal wealth, attitudes to livestock which are wealth-related, environmental deterioration, fuel costs, pressures on land. We cannot neglect these things, but neither can we control or even forecast them with any certainty. They are in the mainstream of evolution, and we shall be swept along in the current, but we can at least try to spare the floods.

Merely staying afloat is a fairly modest ambition and one which recognises the Dyer theory, which I think Jonathon Porritt really gets wrong in his chapter. This theory is the most ultimately utilitarian theory of all. It talks about the confident assumption that life on earth will exist in some form however much we manage to foul things up for our own species and those close to us. So we are not really talking about the survival of the earth, we are talking about the survival of the sort of earth we want. Our limited ambition can, therefore, only be to sustain a reasonable quality of life for ourselves and for those animals that serve us. So the new animal husbandry should be broad in its understanding but modest in its application, and I would cite three things that are required.

One is thrift. Intensification is a good thing, perhaps overdoing it, but it is a good thing. Animals should therefore be used to reduce waste not to create it. This can be done, and I have given you one example, and that is feeding whole crops and by-products to ruminants such as cattle. It could equally be achieved by attaching pig units to supermarkets to harvest the foods that have passed their sell-by date. An equally efficient use of resource.

Point two – compassion. We all have our own personal philosophy as to the rights of animals, but whatever that may be there is now sufficient scientific evidence to demonstrate that all the major farm species have sufficient cognitive powers to recognise quality in life. We are obliged, therefore, to provide, so far as possible, quality and again, so far as possible, quality as perceived by them and not by us.

Final point – realism. Improvements to animal welfare and the environment can only come about if they are perceived by us to have added value, and this means that the animals must continue to work for their living and we must accept the short-term economic consequences of working towards explainable, more humane, agriculture. I began by suggesting that, perhaps in practical terms, animal welfare and the protection of the environment have little in common. In fact, as I have developed this chapter, I realise that within the definition I am using they are exactly the same thing. Again without apology to Jonathon Porritt, I would say we are defining animal welfare as the quality of environment as perceived by the animal and we are defining environment protection as the quality of environment as perceived by us. We are, therefore, concerned with self-interests. However, I would argue that working to ensure quality for our families and other animals may be mere self-interest, but it is enlightened self-interest.

10. Welfare and Conservation

Donald M. Broom

My plan is to consider inter-relations between welfare improvement and the safeguarding of the environment, but first I want to talk about what the term 'welfare' means, and how we can use it in a scientific way.

As a consequence of biological functioning animals have a variety of needs. These needs are met by obtaining a particular resource or by responding to a particular environmental or bodily stimulus. Clearly we need to understand these needs and, in order to do this and in order to understand the responses of animals (and I include man when I say animals) to the difficulties that are encountered during life, we have to understand motivational processes. We have to know about the various behavioural and physiological changes which occur in difficult situations, and we have to understand adverse effects on body condition, growth, reproduction and so on.

Animals have a range of methods of trying to cope and there are various consequences of failure to cope. These are things that we can measure; we can make measurements of the welfare of an animal; the term 'welfare' refers to its state, and its state in particular in respect of its attempts to cope with its environment. One or two points about this concept. The first is that welfare is a characteristic of an individual; it is not something which is given to it by somebody else. The second is that it can obviously vary from very poor to very good, and an individual's welfare will be different at different times. Thirdly, as I said, it can be measured, and it is important that it should be measured in a way that is independent of moral considerations. We have to be able to make measurements of welfare; when we have done that, and discovered how good or poor the welfare is, ethical decisions have to be taken, and individuals will have their own ideas about what is acceptable. The measures which we can use include indications that the animal is failing to cope with its environment (with the difficulties which it encounters) and measures of how hard it is for that individual to cope with the difficulties. So measures of poor welfare include finding that, because of the way an animal is kept or treated, it is not able to live as long or finding that it is not able to grow or is not able to breed. These I think are self-evident; that you can make these measurements and that they are relevant to assessing the welfare of the animal.

Measurements of body damage; for example, if you find that keeping chickens in a particular way results in a large number having broken bones before they die, that is important in assessing the effect of that condition on the welfare of the animal. Measurements of disease-incidence; the welfare of diseased individuals is clearly not as good as that of healthy individuals. The susceptibility of individuals to disease; if animals are kept or treated in such a way that their immune system does not work very well, that in itself tells you that their welfare is less good than it might be. So increased susceptibility to disease is a measure of poor welfare. Then there is a range of measurements of the functioning of the physiological systems of the animal; we can make measurements which tell us how hard a time the animal is having trying to cope with the conditions which are imposed upon it.

There is a range of behavioural methods which animals use to try to cope with the conditions, and again we can make measurements of how much they are having to use these. There are changes in behaviour which are a consequence of the conditions which the animal is having to deal with. A final possibility is that individuals sometimes cope with difficulties by self-narcotising; this is something that is done on a fairly wide scale by man. We would generally feel that the welfare of people who need to knock themselves out with some kind of drug and need to spend a large part of their lives thus self-narcotised is less good than that of people who do not need to. There are indications that self-narcotisation is a method which animals can use to cope with difficulties using endogenous opioids. It may be that in various painful and other unpleasant conditions animals deal with them by an increased usage of endogenous opioids. If so, and if we can measure it (though it is not easy to do so), that again tells us something about their welfare.

Crib-biting is shown a great deal by stabled horses. Pigs often lie down and chew on nothing; they may consume their food in ten minutes during the day. Pigs normally spend a large amount of their day searching for food and consuming food, and pigs which have no food for a long period often exhibit sham-chewing. Pigs which are kept in a fairly barren environment, except for the presence of other pigs, want to chew things, they want to root, but there is nothing to chew on or root so they chew on the tails of other pigs. You can measure the frequency of these sorts of behavioural anomalies.

We can also get some information on how good welfare is by investigating the preferences of animals. We can set up situations – as noted by John Webster – in which we try to find out what is important to the animal by looking at what it prefers and trying to assess how much it will work for something; how important that particular resource is to the animal. Or we look at how strongly animals avoid things, and again that tells us something about how unpleasant the thing is to the animal. So we can use that information as well in assessing how good the welfare of animals is.

I must emphasise, however, that poor welfare and suffering are not exactly synonymous; it is important, I think, to distinguish them in order to understand the concept. They often occur together, but welfare is a wider term than suffering. Marion Dawkins has referred to suffering as 'involving unpleasant subjective feeling'. Now when you have unpleasant subjective feelings there will often be an effect on your state, as regards your attempts to cope with your environment. Unpleasant subjective feelings will be associated with poor welfare. However, it is quite possible for the state of the animal to be affected without there being suffering. For example, an animal may be injured and it may be under anaesthetic; now the welfare of an individual which is under anaesthetic because of the injury – because of the damage to it or perhaps of the reduced life-expectancy – is less good than that of an individual which is not injured. I think that most people would feel that is the right way to use the word, and yet if the animal is anaesthetised it is not suffering. It does not actually feel it, it has not got unpleasant subjective feelings.

Another example is where the immune system is not functioning adequately; suppose we keep animals in a condition which is such that their immune system does not work properly. Now I would say the welfare of those animals is less good because of that; even if they are not being challenged by a disease. If they are, they may suffer directly because of the disease and its effects, but the welfare is less good if the immune system is not working properly. Suppose we think of conditions which lead to impaired reproduction or increased likelihood of mortality. There will be a period where the individual is affected by the condition, but it is not yet suffering. But the welfare has started to decline before the suffering occurs. Suppose we think of individuals which are reared throughout their lives in a situation where there is sensory deprivation. It may be that that individual does not function normally as a consequence of the sensory deprivation. It may be that its functioning is impaired in various ways; perhaps the extent to which it can suffer is impaired by the sensory deprivation. But if there is a substantial enough change in the functioning of the animal we might say that its welfare is poor, even if the animal itself does not detect that its welfare is poor. Finally, if an animal is coping with extremely adverse conditions by self-narcotisation, I would say that its welfare is poor but the effect of the narcotic may mean that it is not suffering. What is the welfare of the drug addict, under the influence of the drug? I would say that, if his life is such that he has to use a drug, the welfare is poor, even if at the moment of using the drug there is no unpleasant subjective feeling. So I would emphasise that it is very valuable to measure suffering; suffering is associated with poor welfare but there can be poor welfare in the absence of suffering.

Now let me consider some of the situations which lead to poor welfare; these have a variety of different effects on animals and I will go over them rapidly. First of all pain; pain is one effect of a situation or an environment on an animal which results in poor welfare. Another is a situation which leads to fear. Again, a situation in which the animal detects that there is danger, or suspects that there might be danger, is something which we need to take account of in considering the welfare of animals.

Then we have a range of measurements where the conflict control systems of animals are not able to work properly; for example, where the animal wants to do something but cannot, or is frustrated. There are situations where an important stimulus is absent and the animal cannot find it; for example, a young animal looking for a teat when there is no teat around. Long periods of insufficient stimulation – extreme boredom, if you like – can result in poor welfare. Over-stimulation, too much unpredictability in the environment, too complex a world which you cannot deal with – that again can be associated with poor welfare.

Having said something about welfare I want now to consider what concern about animal welfare has in common with concern about the environment. The general link has been mentioned several times. There is a basic idea of a moral obligation which we have; a moral obligation towards individual animals with which we come into contact. We have such a moral obligation; most people believe that. We also have moral obligations towards our environment, and there is then this common thread of the feeling of the moral obligation. There is an unselfish element in thinking about this, and we can compare this idea of moral obligation with many of the factors influencing what people do and how they vote. People spend a lot of time thinking about things which are beneficial to themselves; consideration of welfare and the environment has a much larger element of unselfishness in it. Now, if we think about actions which might have a beneficial effect on welfare or on conservation, there are some which benefit both at the same time. Some of our present laws, some laws which could be passed in the future, are also doubly beneficial in this sense.

Here are some examples to start with of actions or laws which improve both animal welfare and the quality of our environment. We have laws which prevent the killing of some wild animals; we have the Badgers Act, we have the Protection of Birds Act. These acts make it an offence to kill these wild animals and they have an obvious effect on conservation; that these animals are not being killed – at least if the law is being obeyed. Also, any attempts to kill wild animals, or almost all attempts, do result in a large amount of suffering. When an animal is shot or caught in a snare, or chased and caught, it has a great deal of suffering. So the welfare of wild animals which are killed is generally rather poor until they die.

A second example is keeping wild animals as pets. If you take any wild animal and keep it in captivity (I would have to say most wild animals; some insects might be taken into captivity without any suffering, but if you take vertebrates into captivity there is certainly going to be suffering), sometimes the animals will die very quickly after being brought into captivity, and again there is often an effect on the functioning of the immune system because they often succumb to diseases which would not otherwise have killed them. So, there is suffering when wild animals are brought into captivity. Collecting animals from the wild and using them as pets has consequences, in many cases which are relevant to conservation. Many wild animals, such as rare parrots, are rare because they are being taken and used as pets. Now in the UK we have laws which prevent most wild birds from being taken and put in a cage. However, many wild animals are caught in other countries and brought into Britain which can then be legally kept. So there is a legal problem here; that we treat our own species in a different way from the way we treat imported wild animals. Generally speaking, this is an area where conservation and welfare tend to go, in most cases, in the same direction.

Another example, and it is a simple one, is using straw on farms. If you use straw as bedding for farm animals, generally speaking you improve the welfare of those animals. Farm animals which are kept in bare pens are generally worse off than farm animals which are kept in pens with straw, both because straw can be used as bedding and because straw is a material which the animal can manipulate. It substantially increases the complexity of the environment of the animal. So using straw can have beneficial effects for our farm animals; burning straw has some direct effects on the environment which are, for the most part, bad as far as conservation is concerned. So straw-burning rather than using straw for animals is something which is bad for the environment and for welfare.

Another example of an issue which has a welfare component

and a conservation component is one which is less important here but very important in many tropical countries: the problem of stray dogs. If dogs are put out from people's houses and left to stray, there is a welfare problem. If dogs survive in the wild, they often have effects on the flora and fauna; so that has a conservation effect and perhaps other effects on species in the environment. Collecting stray dogs is an important measure in relation to conservation, welfare and reducing the spread of human disease. The welfare point is a little complicated, because of course you have to catch up the dogs, and many of those dogs will be killed, but the dogs can be treated well during the time they are held.

There are, then, examples of actions which benefit both welfare and conservation. However, you have heard already of some examples of areas where there is conflict between these two objectives. What one has to do where this conflict is between a welfare aim and a conservation aim is to weigh up all the evidence carefully and decide what is, morally, the right thing to do. It is not realistic to say, 'I'm always going to support anything which improves welfare', or, 'I'm always going to support anything which improves conservation'. You do have to think about both aspects, and many people who are concerned with one area tend to think less about the other area. So, the first example is hunting; animals have been hunted, especially for the purposes of shooting, for many years in this country and there is no doubt that there are large areas of countryside which have been preserved as a consequence of hunting. In other words, conservation has benefited from the existence of hunting.

However, there is also no doubt that if you hunt animals – let's say by shooting them – a high proportion of the animals which are hunted will not die instantaneously. If that happens, if animals are shot and die instantaneously, there is not a welfare problem; there is no interval when the animal is suffering. It is something that many people would not like to see, but there is no question that a high proportion of animals which are shot will carry lead shot for a while, will die after a long period – in many cases days or weeks – and there is a substantial amount of suffering when this happens. The day before yesterday I was in France and I saw people shooting ducks on a lake. A fair proportion of the ducks were obviously hit but carried on and got to a point where the hunters could not pick them up, so a lot of those animals died slowly and in a great deal of pain. This emphasises the point that hunting has adverse effects on the welfare of animals but beneficial effects on conservation, and here there is a conflict of interest. My feeling is that what we ought to do is preserve areas of countryside without having to have this excuse for doing it. There is now a sufficient body of opinion that areas should be conserved without the need for hunting. However, we have to acknowledge the considerable benefits that have accrued in the past because people have hunted – benefits to conservation in general, not to the individual animals being hunted.

Another example is breeding endangered species in zoos. There is no doubt that certain species have been successfully bred in zoos and released in the wild. The number is not that large but there are certainly cases. Captive breeding of rare species is a skill which is developing and which, in the long run, is likely to have a substantial effect on which species do survive. That is something which most people concerned about conservation regard as laudable; it is a worthwhile thing to do. I think the bulk of the British public would say that it is a worthwhile thing to do. However, there is a certain welfare problem when you keep animals in a zoo. The extent of the problem varies a great deal from one species to another. For example, there are species which cannot be bred at all. Quite a number of species cannot breed in captivity, and clearly the welfare of an animal which cannot breed in captivity is by definition not good. So there is an area of conflict here. What is the solution to it? I think the solution is certainly to breed animals in zoos but, if it is done, a great deal of effort must be made to ensure the conditions in which the animals are kept are good, and there are some zoos now which are successful in keeping animals so that their welfare is good. There are many zoos around the world which keep animals in conditions which are very poor, and where there are substantial adverse effects on welfare.

Another problem is the cat. If you have a cat and you let it walk around the countryside rather than confine it in your house; what is the consequence? Well, in many cases the consequence is that the cat chases large numbers of wild creatures; catches, kills and tortures a certain number depending on how efficient it is. So, doing the best you can for the welfare of your cat can have severe adverse effects on the welfare of wild animals. In certain areas, particularly on islands and in places where there are species which are not at all adapted to cope with cats as predators (and that includes the whole of Australia), there have been dramatic adverse effects on populations of a variety of species of small animals because cats are allowed to roam around.

In my view, what should happen here is that cats should not be allowed to roam around in places where they could have a dramatic adverse effect on populations of animals, even though it is better for the cat. Also, if you have a cat and you want to let it out, you could at least provided some sort of warning for the prey, so that the prey has a better chance of escaping; such as a bell around the neck for example. This may be frustrating for the cat – maybe not so good for the welfare of the cat – but it might help to save a fair number of wild animals.

Here is another difficult area which has been mentioned already: housing farm animals. Generally speaking, it is better for farm animals to give them a lot more space and a lot more variety in their environment. However, if we took our present population of farm animals and provided them with free-range conditions, this would have a severe effect on conservation in Britain. We would have to cut down a lot of woodland, we would have to alter our environment substantially, and that is something that people have to bear in mind when advocating free-range. Of course you could say that we do not need all the animals anyway, but at the moment we have got them, so there is a conflict here. For many of these species it is possible to keep them indoors in conditions which are very much better than the average conditions that are used now.

Another area is farming rare species. Crocodiles are being preserved in some parts of the world by farming them, because that means that it is not so worthwhile to go out and kill the wild ones. On the other hand it means the crocodiles have to live on a farm. Elephants: if you actually shoot elephants in a controlled way you may in fact preserve the species, and that is something that has been done, though it is less important if everybody avoids using ivory and it is not worth killing the elephants at all. So for farming rare species: it depends how it is done; avoid it if you can but in some cases it may be necessary.

Finally, I want to say a few words about the problems with our present laws, especially in relation to welfare. I cannot cover all the laws. I thought I would pick out just a few. The major problem with legislation concerning animals is that it is from a human perspective. There ought to be consideration of the animal's perspective when formulating laws; almost all the laws are to protect a certain kind of human interest. They are not designed basically to protect animals and, as has already been mentioned, they depend a great deal upon the use of the animal. The legislation regarding rabbits is extremely different according to whether the rabbit is in a laboratory, is a pet, is being kept for meat or is wild. We have completely different legislation, the rabbits are protected to a completely different extent, according to those circumstances. That is illogical. We ought to have laws which consider the animal as an animal and not just as something that we use in one of fifteen different ways.

The other factor, mentioned by John Webster, is the question of numbers of animals. We have laws in this country about cruelty. Now suppose one considers a farmer who has dairy cows. One of these dairy cows develops severe leg problems to the point where it cannot walk. It collapses onto the ground, which happens to be a deep pile of manure, and it lies there until it is trampled to death by the other cows which are milling continually around it. Now if that happens, the farmer would probably be prosecuted, and yet it is the case that many chickens die in that way every day. We need to modify the way chickens are kept so that this is something which at least is extremely rare; we should try to prevent it completely. The attitudes to the animals are quite different according to the numbers. The reason for that is partly the attitude of the people involved; they will identify with individual cows and know them. The people looking after chickens do not identify with individual chickens and, as has been said already, very large numbers of animals should not be being looked after by very small numbers of people who have no incentive to treat them as individuals.

So, finally, some specific suggestions of changes which could occur in the law:

1. Keeping wild animals as pets. There should be a law that states that no wild-caught animal should be kept as a pet.

That would include animals which are wild coming from other countries. There are difficulties in working out whether the animal is wild or not, but I think we should have a law of that kind. Pets, in other words, should be captive-bred, but you might allow animals which were wild to be brought into a captive-breeding scheme for pet ownership. Wild animals should not be kept as pets at all.

2. The second change concerns cruelty to wild animals. The Protection of Animals Act does not include wild animals. It is quite legal to go out into the countryside, find a hedgehog and pull off its legs one by one. If a policeman observes you doing that he cannot do anything about it because we have no law which makes it illegal to be deliberately cruel to a wild animal. The reason for that is principally to protect people who are hunting; I think that is unreasonable. We should have a law which prevents deliberate cruelty to animals even if those animals are wild.
3. There should be better laws requiring that housing conditions are provided which are sufficient for animals' needs. Animals on farms, in laboratories, in zoos, those kept as pets; there ought to be tighter laws saying what conditions are acceptable. In all those cases there are animals kept in very poor conditions where their needs are not met.
4. At the moment anyone can decide to be a farmer and look after 300 pigs. Nobody can stop someone who knows nothing about pigs from becoming a pig farmer. I think that is wrong; it should be necessary for someone to have a licence in order to keep animals, including keeping animals on farms. That would very much encourage education, the sort of courses which are run by universities, the agricultural colleges, the Agriculture Training Board. These sorts of courses are needed by anyone who keeps animals, and you ought not to be allowed to keep animals unless you have attended such a course. Also, it would be possible to remove a licence from someone who had not looked after animals properly.
5. This point concerns slaughter, which has been mentioned already; however, I would just mention that as far as religious slaughter is concerned, recent research makes it absolutely clear that animals which are killed by cutting

their throats can go for between 15 and 120 seconds able to detect what is going on around them. It is therefore quite unreasonable to allow this; the animals should be stunned at the time the throat is cut. There are various other painful procedures that should be prevented; some laboratory tests on animals, some farm operations etc. We have more information on these now. It should be acted upon, and a number of these practices should be banned.

It is not just a matter of making laws. There has to be better enforcement, and most of all there needs to be better education; everybody in the country needs to hear more about animal welfare and animal conservation from an early age so that they are less likely to do things that have serious adverse effects on animals or the environment.

11. New Thinking is Indivisible

P. D. Wall

When the RSPCA was founded 150 years ago, the abuse of animals was so extreme and obscene that the issues must have appeared simple to the founders. It was not only that animals were suffering to their detriment, but their abusers were themselves brutalised in the process. It must have seemed utterly reasonable to extend the golden rule of the Sermon on the Mount to animals so that animals deserved the same treatment which the human expected from other humans. In a more modern and subtle way, Singer has proposed the same extension of a recognition of interest to animals so that sentient animals share a community of interests with humans. As children, we grow up with the lovely stories in which animals really are people: *The Wind in the Willows, Just so Stories, Watership Down*. As adults, we face the fact that our charming sympathetic introduction to animals becomes more complicated and that we are not fair to ourselves or to the animals if we identify with them. I wish to explore the progress from 1840, with its clear problems and answers, to the present in which we must incorporate much subtler considerations about our relationship with animals and with plants and with the inanimate world about us. I will do so by asking a series of questions.

In what factual sense are we the same as animals?

By factual I mean to question those aspects of us which no longer involve philosophical and theological questions which occupied our ancestors. The first of those facts is that animals and humans are made up of almost identical bits and pieces. We share more than the same atoms and molecules. Individual nerve cells, muscle cells and secreting cells operate on such precisely similar principles that knowledge from one species can be transferred to all others. I know of no religion so fundamentalist as to dispute the facts up to this point. Even beyond this, cells communicate with each other by the same general mechanisms in all animals and plants and even slime moulds. The specific individuality of the species does not appear in their molecules or cells or even in the ability of the cells to communicate with each other during development or in adult life. Individuality resides in the assembly of cells into systems and the precise way in which these systems respond to the world about them. Predators and prey separate in this way. Hawks and pigeons share 99.99 per cent identical components of their cells and of their genetic orders, but the way in which these components are assembled separates the two groups into individual and antagonistic needs and behaviours. Hawks, pigeons and I share an astonishingly similar set of components and mechanisms and we share the same world. I cannot accept that I should adopt a live-and-let-live neutral attitude to hawks and pigeons even though I accept the fact that we share very similar body mechanisms and an identical world. Nor can I accept that it is my duty to reform hawks and pigeons so that they become well-behaved social humans where the hawks stop grabbing baby pigeons and the pigeons stop nicking my peas. How then am I to resolve the morass of conflicting needs and interests of myself and my fellow animals? At a minimum it would seem reasonable to return to the stark simplicity of the RSPCA 150 years ago and agree not to inflict pain on my fellow creatures because pain helps no one and the infliction of it brutalises me. To follow this basic tenet, it would first be necessary to answer an apparently obvious question to which I have devoted much of my life.

How does one recognise pain in an adult human with whom one can speak?

Definition: Judging by the acres of print devoted to a definition of pain, one suspects both an obsession and a difficulty.

Humans often make statements about their awareness of their own internal body state as in 'I am tired; thirsty; hungry; nauseated; drunk; sleepy etc.' These purely subjective announcements do not provoke a debate in which the speaker and listener are challenged to give a precise meaning to the words. Why then do we not take the same laid-back attitude if someone says 'I am in pain … '? I believe the reason is not just that the statement is more dramatic but the nature of the drama. The one who suffers is asking for help. In fact he is asking for two kinds of help: aid to stop ongoing injury and aid to recover from the damage. This call for help provokes a specific urgent reaction and interaction in the listener. For the physician, it is a demand to identify the objective source of the tissue damage which provoked the subjective awareness. Supposing the physician can find no tissue damage or that there is an inappropriate relation between objective fact and subjective complaint. This situation leads to a search for a definition of pain which incorporates the patient's meaning and the physician's ability to respond.

The International Association for the Study of Pain set up a Taxonomy Committee whose first job was to generate an agreed definition of pain.[10] They wrote as follows: 'Pain is an unpleasant sensory and emotional experience associated with actual or potential tissue damage, or described in terms of such damage.' What a weird sentence! This diligent group of doctors and scientists had searched through two thousand years of definitions, added their own considerable experience and had generated a new definition. In an important subscript, they add: 'Pain is always subjective … ' By their definition they had achieved three important end results: (1) the patient is allowed to define the nature of his feelings, (2) the doctor is relieved of the responsibility of finding tissue damage, (3) there is no conceivable way in which a baby or an animal could tell you that it was having an 'unpleasant sensory and emotional experience'. However, since it is proposed that there may be an association between pain and tissue damage, let us examine the facts.

The association of pain in adult man with tissue damage

A very precise lawful and repeated fixed relationship between stimulus and response can be shown in the laboratory. Trained volunteeer subjects who have experienced the stimuli many times and therefore know that no harm will come to them, can give reliable measures of the strength of the stimulus in terms of the strength of their pain perception. Is this not proof that the pain felt by normal subjects mirrors the nature, intensity and location of tissue damage? No! For example there is a local, laboratory, personal, cultural, peer group, arbitrary criterion established for what constitutes a tolerable, i.e. not dangerous, maximal stimulus and response. Therefore these scales vary wildly from laboratory to laboratory.[11] Turning from the laboratory to real life, there is a widely believed myth that battle injuries are not necessarily painful but that injury is always painful in ordinary circumstances. We examined an unselected group of 150 civilians who had suffered accidents sufficiently serious for their admission to hospital.[9] Forty per cent had felt no pain at the time of the accident. They expressed their surprise since they, like the doctors who treated them, associated obvious injury with obvious pain. They were not 'in shock' or confused. A tearful girl with a bomb-shattered leg said, 'Who is going to marry me now', but said she was not in pain. This group were aware of the injury and described it in neutral terms of sensation. They had analgesia precisely localised to the injury. In other words, there was something about the situation in which these people failed to perceive pain in spite of obvious injury whose nature they understood. This group contrasted completely with another 40 per cent who perceived severe pain from the instant of injury and where the severity surprised them and those who treated them. This left only 20 per cent who reported a degree of pain which seemed appropriate to the nature and amount of their injury. We simply do not understand the origin of this hugely variable relation between injury and pain.

We may never fully understand the causal circumstances which produce this bizarre unpredictable relation between abrupt accidents and perceived pain because no one is going to carry out experimental manipulations. We do not need such unthinkable experiments because we are surrounded by thousands of only slightly less dramatic examples of the lack of a fixed relationship between tissue damage and pain. Patients with osteoarthritis have a progressive destruction of joint tissue which can be exactly quantified. They too complain of pain whose severity bears little or no relationship to the tissue destruction. Low back pain patients 'describe their pain in terms of tissue damage' although, in some 80 per cent of cases, no such damage can be detected by the most careful diagnostic tests. This could be explained away by the inadequacy of the diagnosis but that would not restore belief in a fixed relation between pain and damage since we are faced with very large numbers of patients with overt chronic damage and little or no pain. In summary, we can make no general statement on the relation of tissue damage to pain in conscious, sensible adult humans.

Pain measurements by non-verbal methods

Given the wild variability of verbal reports in apparently similar circumstances even when aided by gadgets and gimmicks to translate the words into numbers, there has been an elaborate ongoing search for 'reliable', 'objective' non-verbal measures. Much of this ambition is directed by a simplistic Cartesian dualism with a separated mind from body. Melzack and I and others have written about this extensively.[8] It is classically imagined that there exists direct and reliable neural machinery which detects events in the tissue and transmits the information to a centre where the sensation of pain is generated. The pain centre is observed by the mind which receives the sensory message, minimises or magnifies it, dresses it with memories, significance and emotion, and generates perception with all its quirky infuriating individuality. This simple two-stage process is still the basis of thinking of most of the medical profession and those members of the population who still listen to them. It is the ambition of those who seek a 'real pain'-measuring machine that they should be able to bypass the mind and discover some measuring instrument, a dolorimeter, the equivalent of a thermometer, which could be dipped into the body to measure the true level of pain without reference to that unreliable but verbal witness, the mind. Enormous ingenuity has been mobilised to capture this 'pot of gold'.

The rationale of this Cartesian-Kantian dualism would depend on the following stages of observation:

1. Injury or tissue damage stimulates nerve impulses in specialised sensory fibres.
2. The nerve impulses in these specialised fibres enter the central nervous system and provoke:
   A. Local reflexes in muscles.
   B. Autonomic reflexes affecting blood pressure, heart rate, respiration etc.
   C. Endocrine responses in pituitary, adrenal medulla and cortex etc.
   D. Ascending afferent volleys to thalamus and cortex.
3. The arrival of nerve impulses in thalamus and cortex provoke a 'pure sensation' of pain.
4. The mind assesses the meaning of the pure sensation in terms of the past, present and future and provokes speech and behaviour.
5. Medical treatment reduces the pain.

These five stages are the topic of a huge search by doctors and scientists and are the basis of the rapidly developing new medical speciality of pain diagnosis and management. Unfortunately none of the five provide us with the expected objective measure of pain which we could apply with confidence to adults or to babies or to animals. The basis of the fundamental problem is that most people predict a fixed inevitable hard-wired connection between stimulus and response, between injury and pain. This prediction fails because all of us, humans and animals, are subtle creatures who react to overall situations. Humans are not puppets reacting inevitably to the pulling of one string. Mice are not clockwork mice running around on a course which is the predictable inevitable consequence of some internal machinery. Perhaps the most surprising of these five failures to find an objective measure of pain is the last. It would seem so reasonable to define pain as that verbal response or any other sign which disappears if an adequate dose of morphine is administered. This sounds like a good workmanlike, no-nonsense definition which involves no philosophical meanderings. It could be extended to include any other form of powerful therapy. For example, if surgery were performed to remove all nerves supplying the part from which the complaint originated, this could be used as a test to decide if the word pain could be used to describe the condition which disappeared after the operation. Similarly, cutting pain pathways in the spinal cord or the brain could be utilised as the test procedure which would simply bypass other elaborate ways of defining pain. Unfortunately, there are two huge problems which modify the useful applicability of this pragmatic approach.

Morphine and its related narcotics have proved extremely useful in their ability to control pain. It would seem reasonable to define pain and to measure its intensity in terms of the amount of morphine which a patient freely chooses to take in order to restore his own comfort. I would completely agree provided that this measure applied only to responding patients. It is a great tragedy that there are types of pain which fail to respond to narcotics even when they are given in large repeated doses. These are the truly intractable pains and they are called intractable because they respond to no known form of therapy. They are almost entirely produced by damage to peripheral nerves or to roots or to the central nervous system. In summary, response to therapy may be incorporated in a definition when it works but failure requires other ways of thinking.

How does this paradox apply to animals? Of course, if we observe injury or disease in a human, we attempt to cure it. Of course, if we hear a fellow human complain of pain, we attempt to help. The problem is that many injury and disease states are not apparent to the physician or the patient. Furthermore many serious injury and disease states are not accompanied by inevitable pain. If we have such problems with adult humans with whom we can talk, let us ask the next question.

How does one recognise pain in a newborn baby to whom one cannot speak?

Mothers become great experts in detecting unusual behaviour patterns in their babies. They do not indulge in philosophical debate on pain or the meaning of a cry. They move immediately to the pragmatic therapeutic approach and try to find what action restores the child to normal. The cry of a baby may be associated with hunger, cold, wetness, noise, loneliness, disease and so on. The mother cycles experimentally through her repertoire of restorative therapies such as food, warming, nappy change, lullabies, and cuddling. If these fail and she suspects disease she now incorporates the age-old universal remedies such as massage, heat, cooling, gripe water, aspirin, distraction, and, if those do not succeed, she turns in the West to the doctor.

Until very recently the paediatricians did not concern themselves with pain as such but adopted the direct approach of seeking to locate diseased tissue and to restore that tissue. Now the situation is changing and for the first time two excellent books have appeared on pain in children.[6,7] They naturally concentrate on older children who begin to use words but who need translators and guides so that their words and behaviour are understood by adults and so that the actions of well-intentioned doctors and nurses can be made less threatening to the child. A third book is about to appear dealing with pain specifically in the neonate including premature babies.[1] Here the problem is magnified hugely not only because there are no words but because the behavioural repertoire of the newborn is very limited. This is even more exaggerated in the poorly baby, especially the restricted catheterised premature child in intensive care. Babies who might be in severe pain soon after birth are certain to be severely diseased babies.

In the 1980s, among an entire group of paediatric anaesthetists, a substantial fraction believed that newborn children did not feel pain and therefore they did not give analgesics to newborn babies. I believe these conclusions are based on three erroneous and illogical but well-meaning ways of thinking. First, they were treating babies as adults, that is to say, by a direct attack on the origin of disease with no distraction being permitted to treat symptoms. Symptoms were regarded as mere signposts pointing at the real target. Secondly, they were treating babies as not yet formed adults since their nervous system did not yet contain all the adult structures which they imagined, without any evidence, would be necessary before one could have an unpleasant emotional experience. Thirdly, they had a fearful respect for the dangers of such drugs as morphine and worried that they might kill children who were already desperately sick. No amount of philosophising or, for that matter, sentimentalising will resolve such issues. It is time for direct action, test and observation and I will give two examples which promise a rational future. When a foot is damaged, the volley of nerve impulses produced by the damage and arriving in the spinal cord sets up a long lasting increase of excitability which shows up as an exaggerated flexion reflex, among other changes.[4] Premature babies are routinely subjected to heel lancing in order to obtain blood samples which are needed for crucial reasons. The lanced foot has a grossly exaggerated flexion reflex for days. If a local anaesthetic is rubbed into the skin before the injury, the flexion reflex does not develop its prolonged exaggeration. This very important observation says nothing about whether the baby feels pain. It does show that even a 26-week gestation baby has, at least within its spinal cord, a mechanism which is associated with tenderness in adults. A more serious investigation was carried out on blue babies who required surgery soon after birth to correct congenital heart defects.[2] The outcome was compared in babies operated on with the traditional light general anaesthesia and in those who received analgesics before, during and after the operation. The result was that the babies with analgesia had much reduced postoperative endocrine changes, fewer complications and earlier recovery.

In summary, we do not know and perhaps we can never know if babies experience pain as the word is understood by adults. However, if babies suffer tissue damage for whatever reason, they show fewer behavioural disturbances and recover more quickly if they receive medicine which limits the effect of injury signals.

Therefore is the phrase 'pain in animals' useful?

What have we learnt about the non-verbal correlates of pain in man and babies which might be relevant to animals?

(1) The components

There are those who wish to mechanise man and to assign pain to the operation of a specific Cartesian mechanism whose job is to detect injury and inevitably provoke the pain response. The first component in this classical stimulus-response link is specific injury-detecting nerve fibres, the nociceptors.

Therefore some would say that if an animal has no nociceptors, it cannot feel pain. This is not only simplistic but it is even ignorant of pain-provoking peripheral nerve fibres now known to exist in man. There are those who say that for man to feel pain he must have certain parts of his brain intact such as the spinothalamic tract or the limbic system or the cingulate gyrus etc. Even this is not true. If it were, it would be possible to abolish pain in man by neurosurgical removal of one or more of these structures. This has been the basis of destructive neurosurgery for pain which is now largely abandoned because the pain recurs after some time. The idea that a specific area in the brain is crucial for pain seems no longer valid. Pain in man requires the presence of distributed neuronal circuits rather than a single locus.

Even if the possession of essential components was crucial to man, which it is not, would it be justified to say that an animal which does not have these components could not feel pain? We have seen that argument applied to babies. I believe such a statement would involve an outdated phrenological approach which implied that the brain was a collection of specifically labelled boxes. The function of nerve fibres is to transmit coded information from one place to the other. As humans we can transmit messages to each other by speaking, writing, morse code, semaphore and smoke signals. There is every reason to believe that nerve fibres can also transmit messages from cell to cell with different codes. Therefore, if we cannot detect a particular coded message in an animal, there is no reason to say that they are not transmitting the particular message by some other means. Similarly, nerve cells with their dendrites and synapses are logic units. These can modify their operation to detect temporal and spatial patterns of inputs. Certainly a cockroach has enough such components to detect the relatively simple set of circumstances we call painful.

(2) The reflexes

We have seen that the reflexes in man whether muscular, autonomic or endocrine are components of our reaction to injury. They are usually coupled with pain but that correlation is too loose for reliability. Furthermore they show the same variation of response in relation to injury which is also seen in general behaviour and in verbal declarations of pain.

(3) Behaviour

'Sentient animals' is a favourite phrase of those who wish us to extend our obligations beyond our fellow men to include animals. I consider this phrase an anthropomorphic trap. The intent is to define some wide group of animals – say, mammals or vertebrates – as sentient and therefore capable of feeling pain. I am not comfortable with these arbitrary limits. I strongly suspect the limits are set by social empathy in interactions with animals. Beyond the vertebrates, I confess to my own failure to have social relations with snails but to my deep and, I suspect, mutual respect for the octopus which is a close relation of the snail. The role of social relations is obvious in the massive US Animal Welfare Act 1966 which applies to warm-blooded animals, thereby excluding my friend the octopus. However, by 1977 this act was further amended by excluding rats, mice, birds, horses and farm animals from the definition of animal. Well, well! It would seem that there are two types of warm-blooded animal. One lot live on farms and the rest deserve welfare. By 1989, the City Council of Cambridge, Mass., extended protection to all vertebrates. One suspects the farm lobby is pretty weak in Cambridge, but so is the invertebrate lobby. What about the 'Sensitive Mimosa' which has its own version of the flexion reflex so that flicking one leaf collapses all the leaves on that branch? Why is that not sentient? I find all this uncomfortably arbitrary. Am I to base my ethical values on the warmth and nature of my social relations? That did not work too well for blacks, slaves and even women. Why should I require animals to join me in some mutual admiration society or even make them honorary members? Perhaps like Groucho Marx they have other views about exclusive clubs. Groucho said, 'Any club that would accept me as a member, I wouldn't want to join.'

Beyond the issue of the meaning of sentience, we have seen that the relation of injury to pain and its associated behaviours is highly variable in man. If one were to follow Descartes and attribute that variability to the mind, then animals who were mindless in the opinion of Descartes and Kant would react reliably and predictably to injury. If this were so, an examination of an animal for pain-related behaviour would be as good as asking the animal if it was in pain. Furthermore, the observation of pain-related behaviour would be a reliable indication of injury or tissue damage in such a mechanical, mindless animal. That this is not so is very apparent from any number of reports which cannot be dismissed as anecdotage. The 1980 Epsom Derby was won in fast time by the horse Henbit. Three hundred metres from the end of the race, the horse stumbled and fractured its right fore cannon bone. It then accelerated out of the pack and passed the finishing post placing full weight on the fractured leg in a perfect gallop gait. When a pack of fox hounds in full bay pour through a barbed wire fence, they leave long bleeding lacerations on their sides. The injured dogs' behaviour cannot be differentiated from that of their uninjured pack mates. I have described elsewhere similar behaviour in wounded deer.[12] Most dog owners have had the misfortune to see it in their own pets in a dog fight. The variable response to acute injury in such animals is reminiscent of the variability we have described for humans. The similarity continues if people or animals are examined at a later stage. Henbit would never approach the winning speed again. Wounded deer by the next day separate from the herd and fail to groom or eat or move. Dogs lie 'doggo'. In summary, pain-related behaviours in animals and in humans may be triggered by injury, but the intensity and latency of these behaviours depends on many circumstances other than injury.

A characteristic of human verbal expression of pain is that it contains a mixture of private suffering and public display. There is no reason to doubt that such mixtures of behaviour would not occur in social animals. It could be threatening to the group or at least bad manners for a lion or a wolf or a hyena to yelp and limp on twisting an ankle during a communal stalk. Normally noisy monkeys are unusually quiet during childbirth, perhaps because they are particularly vulnerable to predators when in labour.[5] It would seem highly probable that animals like humans would take into account the presence of other animals when displaying signs of tissue damage. If you watch the jamboree of the many species which gathers at a lion kill, you observe that each animal changes its normal behaviour. Normally obsessionally dignified storks become instant hooligans. Nowhere is this shift of behaviour more dramatic than in courting rituals. It is my contention, by analogy with man, that the sensory world of these animals will shift as they move from one item to another in their behavioural repertoire. If this were so, it would be as meaningless to make general statements about what a mouse or a cock or a cobra feels as it is to generalise about human behaviour. It would be necessary to understand the particular animal's relation to its environment at the particular time.

(4) Response to analgesic therapy

We have seen how useful it can be to define human pain as that state which disappears if the human is treated for pain. It would seem reasonable to call a drug an analgesic for a rat if it delays the time when the rat licks its feet when parked on a hot plate. In a real disease state rather than an artificial provocation, it is necessary to examine very carefully the animal's disease behaviour and then its response to treatment. For example, in a rat-form of rheumatoid arthritis a very careful study of the ameliorating effect of narcotics showed that the animal's scratching was the most strongly affected abnormal behaviour.[3] Without that careful study, scratching would not normally be considered a sign associated with arthritis.

In assessing the effect of an anti-pain therapy, it is obviously important but difficult to be certain that the treatment has not simply prevented the animal from displaying the sign. The extreme example of this would be to paralyse the animal, which would increase the pain and terror of a man even though he was unable to display any sign of pain. We must be aware that paralysis of sign could occur in a more subtle fashion. For example, it is common veterinary practice to section the nerves to the hoof of a limping horse. This is not done in man because it leads to Charcot joints and a deafferentation phantom, two signs the horse may not be able to display.

Therapy is not a guaranteed test in humans because there are intractable pains which fail to respond to any known therapy. There is no reason to think that similar conditions would not exist in animals. Furthermore, because of the differing neurotransmitters and structures and behavioural repertoires, it could be that effective analgesics for humans are not necessarily effective in all animals.

Finally, we have seen in humans that the assessment of specific therapies is always complicated by the presence of the placebo response. It is true that, for us, this is usually a highly sophisticated learnt response. We grow up to believe that doctors in white coats prescribe effective pain-relieving tablets and if the situation is serious they give intravenous injections. The consequence is that we have placebo responses to blank tablets and much stronger placebo responses to intravenous injections of saline which we are told is some new wonder drug. Obviously, animals have no such sophistication and, just as babies, fail to respond to these placebos. However, there is no reason to believe that behaviour cannot be switched by simpler means such as false cues. For example, we know that rats respond to 'nocebos'. If a rat is placed in a marked box and given an injection of apomorphine, it sits still for half an hour with its hair erect and shivering. If, six months later, it is placed in the same box and given an injection of saline, it displays the identical behaviour as when given the drug. By false cues and by real cues lumped under the general title 'distraction', we may shift the behaviour of adults, babies and animals.

In summary, the assessment of pain in babies and animals is so much more difficult than in adult humans that we must face the likelihood that we often get it wrong. The difficulty extends far beyond the lack of verbal language for four reasons. First, we have no reason to associate pain with the possession of any one neural component. Secondly, reflex responses are parts of overall behavioural responses and may be uncoupled in particular situations. Thirdly, overall behavioural responses require for their observation an intimate familiarity with each species which is rarely achieved and could be unachievable. Lastly, animal response to analgesic therapy designed for humans can be an excellent criterion when the animal responds but the failures which mark the intractable pains of man could be more common in animals.

An alternative approach

I trust I have provided enough reasons to show that the use of the phrase 'pain in animals' is so indefinable that it is meaningless to animals and to those who have the well-being of animals at heart. The misunderstandings of 'pain in animals' can work to the severe detriment of the animals by attempting to assign to them specifically human values. What might be a set of values which could be useful? For the individual animal within itself, we could propose, with Claude Bernard, that each individual seeks to regulate its internal environment which is a crucial condition for its free life. Instead of agonising over an indefinable concept of pain, why do we not simply study the individual's efforts to stabilise its internal environment and then aid it or, at least, not intrude on those efforts without good reason? But the animal also lives in an external environment and we have here a fundamental new set of ethical values being developed by the ecologists and 'green' people. We are now beginning new ways of thinking about whether to feed mice or kill them, plant trees or chop them down which require new balances of conflict of interest. Rodents have a value on the world scene, but is that value sufficient to give them permission to eat 20 per cent of the grain harvest of India? Snakes, locusts, bacteria and viruses are welcome to occupy their valuable niches in our world but they do go over the top on occasions. It is our human duty and pleasure to understand the locust as a locust but we are equally morally compelled to find ways to control their self-destructive rampages. I firmly believe that if we study animals as animals including their struggles with their internal and external environments, we can liberate them and ourselves from the obfuscation of terms such as pain and turn instead to definable values. A search for those values will not only permit deep thought and research, it will demand and support it.

References

1. Neonatal pain and distress, In: *Pain Research & Clinical Management*, vol. 2, ed. K.J.S. Anand & P.A. McGrath (1991), Elsevier, Amsterdam.
2. Anand, K.J.S., Sippell, W.G. & A. Aynsley-Green (1987) Randomized trial of fentanyl anaesthesia in preterm babies undergoing surgery. *Lancet* 1: 243-7.
3. DeCastro, C., DeSutter, P., Gybels, J. & von Hees, J. (1981) Adjuvant arthritis in rats. *Pain* 10: 173-85.
4. Fitzgerald, M. (1987) Pain and analgesia in neonates. *Trends in Neuroscience* 10: 344-6.

5. Lefebre, L. & Carli, G. (1985) Parturition in non-human primates. *Pain* 21: 315-27.
6. McGrath, P.A. (1990) *Pain in Children*. Guildford, New York.
7. McGrath, P.J. & Unruh, A.M. (1987) *Pain in Children and Adolescents*. Elsevier, Amsterdam.
8. Melzack, R. & Wall, P.D. (1988) *The Challenge of Pain*, 2nd edition. Penguin, London.
9. Melzack, R., Wall, P.D. & Ty, T.C. (1982) Acute pain in an emergency clinic. *Pain* 14: 33-43.
10. Merskey, H. (1983) Classification of chronic pain. *Pain* Suppl. 3: 1-225.
11. Sternbach, R.A. & Turksy, B. (1964). On the psychophysical power function in electric shock. *Psychosom. Sci*. 1: 217-18.
12. Wall, P.D. (1979). On the relation of injury to pain. *Pain* 6: 253-64.

12. Our Closest Living Relatives

Jane Goodall

The continuing research into the behaviour of free-living chimpanzees in Gombe National Park began in 1960. This makes it the longest unbroken study of a wild animal group anywhere in the world. Gradually, over the years, I have gained an ever-deeper understanding of chimpanzee nature. This has given me a deep commitment not only to the species as a whole and its survival in the African forests, but also to individuals in captivity around the world.

Many aspects of chimpanzee behaviour are similar to our own. Chimpanzees have a long childhood, and they have close family bonds that may endure throughout a life of up to 50 years. One family, in particular, has taught me a great deal. In 1964 the old matriarch Flo had a known family of four – infant Flint, juvenile Fifi, adolescent Figan and the young adult male Faben. When Fifi was about 13 years old she gave birth to her first infant. Possibly as a result of Flo's extreme age (we suspect she was nigh on 50 when she died) Flint developed an abnormally dependent relationship with his mother. When she died, Flint, although he was over 8 years old, seemed unable to survive without her. He quickly developed signs of clinical depression such as may be observed in socially deprived human children. In this state of grieving, his immune system weakened, he became sick of some intestinal disease and died about a month after Flo.

Fifi, like Flo before her, was a good mother – patient, tolerant, affectionate and playful. Young chimpanzees learn a great deal during childhood, just as our children do. They must learn, for example, the different tool-using traditions of their own particular community. We now know that these traditions, or cultures, differ in different populations across Africa. There is much to learn too as regards social etiquette.

Young chimpanzees are acrobatic and playful, filled with energy. In the wild there is always plenty for the youngsters to do. They can be very innovative in their games; they play with objects just as our children play with toys. One infant invented a game with sand – the challenge seemed to be to get as much as he could in his mouth while getting none in his eyes. If there are no other chimpanzee youngsters to play with, sometimes there is a young baboon. There are many baboons at Gombe, and often friendships form between individual youngsters. Freud often played with Hector.

The mother intensifies her efforts to wean her child during the fourth year. All youngsters go through what we call *weaning depression*, when the frequency of play drops and the child spends increased time in contact with the mother. But by the time the next infant is born, when the older child is about 5 years, weaning is usually complete. However, he or she remains emotionally dependent on the mother and is by no means cast out of the family group. This is how long-term bonds can develop between family members. For the second child, growing up is very different from what it is for a first-born – for the elder sibling serves as a built-in playmate, someone who is almost always ready to join in a game even if the mother is not in the mood.

We have followed the history of many families at Gombe and recorded the gradual development of close friendly relations between the various individuals. We have seen how young adult males like Goblin continue to travel with their mothers, each reassuring the other during tense moments. We have recorded how Goblin would hasten to help not only his mother but his adult sister. And we have now observed many cases when infants, whose mothers died, were adopted and cared for by older individuals; usually their elder siblings, but once a non-related adolescent male.

The long-term outlook for the 150 or so chimpanzees at Gombe is grim. Cultivation has crept right up to the boundaries of the 30-square-mile national park – very small by Tanzanian standards. The three communities of chimpanzees are thus virtually imprisoned and can no longer exchange genetic material with neighbouring chimpanzee groups.

Nevertheless, the Gombe chimps live in a paradise compared with many of those over much of the rest of their range. They extend across Africa, mainly in the equatorial belt, from the west coast to western Tanzania and Uganda in the east. Once these apes were present in twenty-five African nations; they have totally gone from four, they are on the verge of extinction in five more; and only four countries in the central part of their range – Cameroon, Gabon, Congo and Zaire – support significant populations. At the turn of the century chimpanzees existed in hundreds of thousands – today there are unlikely to be more than 250,000 remaining, and the rate of decline is accelerating.

Chimpanzees are vanishing because of habitat destruction, either clear-cutting for agriculture and human dwellings, or logging. The logging companies go deeper and deeper into the forests, not only destroying the trees but opening up the area for hunters and settlers, and taking with them human diseases. Chimpanzees are susceptible to all known human infectious diseases (except cholera).

Chimpanzees are also disappearing because of hunting; in some African countries they are hunted for food, and in most parts of their range, even if chimp flesh is not eaten, mothers are selectively shot so that their infants can be stolen from their dead or dying bodies and sold. They may be sold in the country of origin, as pets, or to dealers who resell them, usually for a huge profit, for the international entertainment and biomedical industries. Today this export from Africa is usually illegal.

This method of catching infants is not only cruel, it is also incredibly wasteful. You can imagine a hunter, usually using a primitive and inefficient weapon, shooting a mother who is only wounded. She creeps away and dies from her wounds; her infant will almost certainly die also. Other chimpanzees may try to defend mother and child; they may be shot and wounded or killed. Sometimes an infant will be killed at the same time as its mother. And even if one is successfully captured, he or she may die on the long journey from the place where his mother was shot to his final destination in Africa. These transports from the forest to the dealer camps, or the market, are, in most cases, a nightmare. The infant, terrified and hurting, will typically have hands and ankles tied with rope or wire and, in addition, be pushed into a small crate, or sack. I have seen the results of such treatment – deep cuts and sores. And they are seldom given proper food. It is not surprising that many are dead on arrival. Even if they survive the journey, dealer camps are notoriously bad; there is usually nobody there who understands their needs.

Some of the young chimpanzees who do survive become pets; many of these are bought by Europeans sympathising with their plight. For a while, if their owners are caring and understanding, they may enjoy their lives, unnatural though they are. For a few years they will probably be given the run of house and garden, live as part of the family. But by the time they reach 5 or 6, at the latest 7 years, they become potentially dangerous. They are inventive, highly intelligent, and destructive. They resent discipline. It is no longer practical or safe to allow them loose. And so for a second time their freedom is taken away.

Socrates was about 5 years old when I first met him and he had lived for over a year in a tiny cage, in which he could barely turn around, in someone's backyard in Burundi. Whiskey, whom I also encountered in Burundi, was older; he had been living for two years on the end of a two foot chain in what was once a lavatory at the back of an Arab's garage.

Gregoire was captured in 1944 and put into the Brazzaville zoo when it first opened. He may be one of the oldest zoo chimps there is. When I first met him he was like a skeleton, and almost hairless. Most zoos in economically poor African countres do not provide good conditions for their animals. And chimpanzees and monkeys, unfortunately for them, like the same kind of food as humans. Because there is so much poverty among the people of Zaire, and because Gregoire's keepers could not afford more than one meal a day, it was scarcely surprising that some of the oranges and bananas intended for the animals found their way to their keepers' families.

Charlie is one of the chimpanzees rescued from Spain. Most people today are aware of the Beach Chimp racket. Infant chimpanzees, many from Equatorial Guinea, are smuggled into Spain and the Canary Islands. There they are dressed up in inappropriate clothes, dragged around in the sun, forced into the noisy, smoky nightclubs in the evening, and, to keep them docile, heavily drugged. Tourists are persuaded to have their photographs taken holding these pathetic youngsters. By the time they are six or seven they have usually had their teeth knocked out, but even so they are becoming large and potentially dangerous. At one time they were then killed. Today it is more likely that they are smuggled out of Spain, perhaps through Austria or other parts of eastern Europe, destined for biomedical research. We used to think that these youngsters were dosed with Valium, or some similar tranquilliser. But Simon and Peggy Templer, who set up a rescue station for confiscated chimps in Spain, have reported horrifying withdrawal symptoms in some of the youngsters they have rehabilitated. Charlie was darted to anaesthetise him for his journey to a sanctuary in the UK (Monkey World). To my amazement he pulled out the dart, examined it and then, quite clearly, tried to give himself a fix. When the needle fell off he brought the whole thing to me, put it in my hand, and turned his shoulder. Clearly he, like so many other youngsters in the trade, had been hooked on hard drugs.

Some chimpanzees end up in biomedical research laboratories. Until last year, SEMA Inc, in Rockville, Maryland, was one of the worst in the USA. When I visited, I saw pairs of two-year-old chimps being kept in quarantine in cages 22 × 22 ins, and 24 ins tall. Each cage was inside a sort of metal box, like a microwave oven which, except for a tiny glass window, excluded all contact with the outside world. These cages were stacked one on top of the other, in room after room. After quarantine they were separated, and each placed alone in a very slightly larger cage, also in an 'isolette'. And there they stayed, in totally sterile, barren environments, for up to three years. During that time most of them became insane. Recently these cages have been discarded. Thanks to the efforts of animal welfare groups, the cages are now much larger in a facility that has been totally rebuilt. But they are still housed alone. They can see each other, but they cannot hear each other. And we must remember that the emotional needs of a chimpanzee infant are similar – perhaps identical – to those of a small human child. There is, for both, a desperate need for love and reassurance.

What is so shocking is that the legally accepted minimum

cage size in America for a fully adult chimpanzee – our closest living relative – is 5 ft by 5 ft, and 7 ft high. In one lab, LEMSIP – part of the New York University Medical School – there are over 300 chimpanzees in conditions of this sort.

Things, admittedly, are somewhat better in other labs, such as TNO in Holland, where the chimpanzees are, for the most part, maintained in social groups. Even experimental individuals are almost always caged in pairs. But their cages are bleak, and young ones removed from their mothers were, when I visited, crowded into an inappropriate wire prison. And there are better conditions, too, in some of the American labs such as the Southwest Biomedical Foundation, and Bastrop, both in Texas.

We do not use chimpanzees for medical research in the UK, but let us not be hypocritical – our scientists, if they feel it necessary to use chimpanzees, use those in Holland or America. And many of us use drugs or vaccines that have been tested on chimpanzees.

After working with chimpanzees for thirty years I have learned a good deal, not only about the ape's place in nature, but about our own as well. In many ways this is very humbling because an understanding of chimpanzee behaviour and intellect and emotion – like our own in so many ways – makes us realise that we are not as unique, as a species, as we used to think. We are not standing on a pinnacle, separated from the rest of the animal kingdom by an unbridgeable chasm. As yet, most people do not appreciate the extent to which recent scientific knowledge has served to blur the line, once thought to be so definitive, between human and non-human animals. In this way the chimpanzee, I believe, can greatly help the animal welfare movement. Understanding the closeness that exists, in so many spheres, between ourselves and the great apes helps us to bridge the imagined gap between 'man' and 'beast'. This should lead to a new awareness, a new respect, for all the other wonderful non-human beings with whom we share the planet.

Once we have learned to respect all life forms, what should we do about the obvious cruelties and injustices that we see all around? In particular, what am I trying to do for the species that has given me so much during the past thirty years? We have formed the Jane Goodall Institute (in UK, USA, Canada and Tanzania) specifically to fight for the well being of chimpanzees. In Africa, in Burundi, Congo and Angola, we are building sanctuaries for the chimpanzees whose mothers were shot and whose owners could no longer cope. In Burundi a total of 13 young chimpanzees, including Socrates and Whiskey, await the construction of a large enclosure in which they can live in a social group, climb trees and feel the sunshine. We have gathered them all together in what we call the Half Way House where they have spacious joined cages and are getting to know each other and play again.

Gombe, as I mentioned, is now an island of forest surrounded by cultivation. That the chimpanzees are safe from poaching is largely due to the interest of the local people. We employ Tanzanians from the villages surrounding the park, not to perform menial jobs, not for tracking or patrolling, but actually to study the chimpanzees, recording their behaviour in writing and 8mm video. They are proud of their work, and they are fascinated by and care about the chimpanzees. They go back to their villages and talk about them to their families and friends. They would not tolerate anyone who tried to kill their chimpanzees. We hope to export this conservation strategy to other African countries. We are starting a project in Burundi – with the approval of the Government – in one of the few forests left. We are training chimpanzee researchers from among the local Burundi people. And we are planning to do the same thing in the Congo, in one of the forested areas on the west coast. There we hope to train some of the best hunters to use video cameras, then pay them more for their footage than they would get if they shot with guns and sold the animals for food. We have to remember, always, that no conservation efforts will work unless the local people are involved in meaningful ways, and unless the government is convinced that there are alternatives to hunting and selling trees for timber.

There are, fortunately, some wonderful people helping in the battle to help chimpanzees. I have mentioned Simon and Peggy Templer, the British couple in Spain, who fought so hard and successfully to get Spanish law changed and the use of chimpanzees on the beaches outlawed. In Zambia there is another remarkable British couple, Dave and Sheila Siddle. They have created a wonderful sanctuary which now houses more than 30 chimpanzees, some confiscated by the Zambian government, some sent to the Siddles by people from all over the world who have been concerned about the plight of individual chimpanzees. The RSCPA made a donation to enable the completion of a new enclosure where they can start a second chimpanzee group.

What about the labs? What are we doing to help the 'prisoners of science' behind their steel bars and locked basement doors? Of course, they should not be in the labs at all. But they are there, and there for a while they will stay, tools in the search to understand and cure our own diseases. Should we abandon them, hoping merely that things will get better as more and more alternatives to the use of living animals are found and fewer and fewer chimpanzees are needed? Hoping that, eventually, none will be used at all. Or should we try to do something for the individuals who are there *now*? We feel it is necessary to try to alleviate the tremendous psychological suffering of the 1,500 or so chimpanzees in labs across the United States. There are another 50 in Holland, another 50 in Austria, and many more, in smaller groups, in various countries around the world. The JGI-USA has sent a student into one of the labs to enrich the lives of the inmates. And to work with the technicians. The chimpanzees now have various tasks to perform to occupy themselves during the long hours of each day. It is poignant to see the excitement shown when their boredom is alleviated by a simple procedure – such as arrival of a popcorn machine. Many ideas have now been tried, some more successful than others. We are putting all this – which is used in the zoos as well – into a book.

We do see change – as described for SEMA, Inc. But it is much too slow.

What about zoos? There are still many really bad zoos, even in the UK. And in Europe, and in America where the roadside zoo and circus is still popular in some states. One JGI programme is ChimpanZoo. In 16 zoos in the USA students, keepers and volunteers are studying groups of chimpanzees and providing enrichment in their lives. I believe this programme will soon be international. And what of zoos in Africa? In Congo Brazzaville we have hugely improved conditions in the zoo – with a good deal of help from the RSCPA. Gregoire is quite plump, has grown a lot of hair, and has a chimpanzee companion in the next door cage. They can (and do) touch through the bars. We plan to build a large outdoor enclosure for him and the other zoo chimpanzees, and an orphanage for other infants that, from time to time, are confiscated from hunters coming down the river from the still wild forests of the north.

Let me end with a story about a chimpanzee in a zoo. In 1990 the Detroit zoo opened the largest chimpanzee exhibit in north America. It was surrounded by a moat (chimpanzees cannot swim). Chimpanzees were selected from zoos around the world so that there would be a good deal of genetic diversity in the new group. When the various individuals were introduced to each other there were, as would be expected, a number of quite fierce fights. During one of these early skirmishes a female fled into the water and drowned. The exhibit was closed and a safety bar put up to prevent further tragedies.

Some weeks later the No. 2 male, Jojo, was attacked by the new top-ranking male and he too fled into the moat. He crossed the safety bar, floundered in the deep water beyond, and began to sink. There were some people standing on the far side of the moat, including some keepers. They were afraid to go into the water but, luckily for Jojo, there was a truck driver, Rick Swope, who was there with his family. As Jojo sank for the third time Rick jumped in. The zoo staff yelled at him to get out, but he ignored them. The water was muddy after rain, and he had to swim under water, feeling with his hands. Presently he felt the chimpanzee's inert body, managed to lift him out of the water, and got him over the safety bar. But when he pushed him up onto the bank the slope was such that Jojo began to slip back into the water. At this point other chimpanzees, hair bristling, screaming, charged towards the scene. The people on the bank yelled even louder at Rick, telling him to 'let the monkey drown!' But Rick, despite the fierce approach of other chimpanzees, pushed Jojo back up and held him there until he raised his head, took a few groggy steps, and collapsed onto level ground. Rick, without doubt, saved his life.

The director of JGI-USA called up Rick when he read about the incident in the papers. He asked him 'Why did you do that, Rick? You knew it was dangerous?' 'Well, I looked into his eyes, and it was like looking into the eyes of a man, and the message was: Won't anybody help me?'

That is the kind of action that can make us proud of being

human. And it is symbolic, too. It is a story we can remember when we are standing, like Rick, on the brink of muddy water. Will we stand there and watch, like the zoo staff, or, like Rick, jump in and try to help?

13. A New Technology: Genetic Engineering

Michael Fox

We are on the threshold of a new technology: Genetic Engineering/Bio-technology. Not much is known about it by the general public. There are a lot of irrational fears and a lot of great promises, many of which are not founded in terms of how humanity could benefit from the genetic engineering of animals, plants and micro-organisms.

First, a brief background. We have tried to bring about a moratorium in the United States on the patenting of animals. The US Patent and Trade Mark Office decided in 1986 to allow the patenting of all genetically engineered creatures, everything except human beings because we are ostensibly protected under the Constitution. This decision was based upon a narrowly won ruling by the Supreme Court in a hearing over a micro-organism that had been genetically engineered. The Supreme Court said, 'Yes, micro-organisms can be patented.' The US Patent Office extended this ruling to embrace all creatures: warm blooded, cold blooded, the lot. We were very concerned about this, and we called the ruling arbitrary and capricious because it was done without any public debate whatsoever. The Government agencies are supposed to serve the public interest. They are supposed to act upon instruction and initiative from Congress through direct congressional mandate or congressional legislation, but they made a public policy decision of potentially profound ramifications for the rest of time without any public debate; so we tried for a moratorium. And the way things stand now there is legislation in the House and in the Senate to pull for a two-to-five-year moratorium, so there can be more public debate against this technology in terms of animal protection, environmental and other concerns, which I shall review.

But one of the Chairmen of the key committees drafted legislation which may go through at the next round of Congress when they return in September. And there was a clause in that to the effect that all farmers would have to pay a royalty or user fee to the companies that held the patent rights on engineered farm animals; and the farmers did not want this, of course, which created a log-jam. They were getting nowhere with the legislation, and the bio-technology industry has now caved in and said, 'Okay, farmers, you don't have to pay a user fee.' So with this opening, I have a feeling that there will be less of a rush towards developing patentable farm animals for pure production, but there will be a significant rush in other areas of patenting animals for the bio-medical research area and pharmaceutical farming which I shall be talking about shortly.

So when we look at this bio-technology we must consider ethical, environmental and animal welfare concerns. Basically, the integrity and future of creation are in our hands now. We have power over the genes of life. As with any new technology there are risks and benefits and it could be a Pandora's Box. Remember that the last element in Pandora's Box was hope.

One of our first concerns is the environmental impact, the so-called domino effect. If genetically engineered organisms, micro-organisms or macro-organisms, are released into the environment, we have no science of environmental prediction; so there are inherent risks here. One could be the spraying, for example, of a bacillus to kill certain insect parasites on various mono crops. The alternative agriculture scientists would say that this would not be the right approach. Why are there pest problems to begin with? Because you are practising a type of agriculture, such as raising just one species of tree, that is essential in making these trees highly susceptible to harmful insects. With a diversity of trees you have a diversity of insects, you have a diversity of birds and so on, which helps keep things in balance. So when you have a mono-culture you create pests. So is this an appropriate response by technology? I doubt it.

When we look at some of the developments in the agriculture sector we find that several companies, like Monsanto and Eli Lilly, have developed genetically engineered seeds that are resistant to herbicides, so the farmer can pour the herbicides on to his fields and only these seeds will grow. It is a very nice package deal because Monsanto and Eli Lilly and so on are manufacturing specific pesticides as well as selling seeds, so it is a splendid game of Monopoly. But is this the kind of agriculture we want? What we urgently need in the developed, industrialised world is a sustainable agriculture which does not poison the entire food chain. That helps to enhance bio-diversity. Now the genetic engineers are saying, 'Oh well, bio-technology will enhance bio-diversity because we can change the genetic structure.' But they are monkeying around with the utility species of corns, pigs and so on which are primarily being used in intensive agriculture practices. The rare breeds, the rare varieties of seeds, are virtually not being looked at. So there are some serious problems in terms of reducing bio-diversity as well as the diversity of farming practices. Having plants that produce various toxins out of the roots to kill insect pests could also be hazardous, because if we do harm to the micro-organisms in the soil with excessive use of fertilisers and herbicides we finish up with dead soil. Some of the agriculture analysts will show you fields in the United States – for example, in California where they grow vast amounts of tomatoes and other crops to ship all over the country – where the soil is dead. The soil is simply used to hold the plant up; hence the need for more pesticides and more fertilisers. When you put more fertilisers into the soil – synthetic fertilisers – it weakens the plant immune systems to insect pests and so on; so you then need more pesticides. And this is wonderful for the petro-chemical, pharmaceutical, industrial complex. It is the petro-chemical, pharmaceutical, industrial complex that is at the forefront of these new developments in genetic engineering bio-technology, seeking monopoly of world germplasm and essentially maintaining the status quo of ecologically unsound and inhumane farm animal practices.

One of Monsanto's creations is the caterpillar surprise. Tomato plants were stripped by caterpillars in the Monsanto lab but those with an inserted gene that produces a toxin repelled the pests. Is this progressive? No, because modern agriculture can create pests. We farm differently. We don't have pests, or when you do have occasional eruptions you use pesticides and ways of controlling disease in gentler ways.

It is possible to inoculate steers with recombinant rinderpest vaccine. This is a genetically engineered vaccine developed by the US Department of Agriculture. The vaccine was developed by placing two rinderpest virus genes into the vaccine phial of the smallpox virus. Now this sounds wonderful when we think of the Third World where this rinderpest disease, especially in East Africa, is extremely common. Livestock are riddled with the disease and with many others, but is this the way to go – when overgrazing and overstocking is a serious problem in many Third World countries and also in parts of the United States?

In the world today we have 1.2 billion cattle, 1.6 billion sheep and goats and 800 million pigs and 5.3 billion people. If we are concerned about wildlife and wild lands we need to reduce this population of farm animals and integrate that population with a sustainable way of using range land and of raising and recycling crops primarily used for human consumption. Vegetarianism is one answer, but it is not an appropriate response to a world community that still wants meat and a world community of poor who aspire to eat meat. So we are working with some producer organisations in the United States, organic farming associations and the like, to develop a humane sustainable agriculture with recommended codes and guidelines for various husbandry practices, with the idea of a green heart label that indicates to the conscientious consumer, the non-vegetarian conscientious consumer, that this animal has been raised humanely, that it has not had growth stimulants or antibiotic stimulating drugs in the feed, and has been produced in an ecologically sound way.

One of the most serious problems facing animal agriculture today, which bio-technology is not going to help, is the vast volume of animal waste. An egg city of one million laying hens will produce about as much waste as a town of about 30,000 people. Where is it all going? It seeps into the ground water and is a serious source of contamination of drinking water. There are trace elements and additives in this waste, like arsenic and copper, that are further environmental hazards.

Then we have the contribution to acid rain from some of the gases from animal waste and the contribution to global warming from carbon dioxide, and especially from methane. And then, in raising crops for farm animals and in clearing land to give them more forage, we engage in deforestation, which accelerates global warming too.

Every nation state needs to address the impact of its livestock agricultural practices on the environment. Livestock accountability is essential. It is as essential today as environmental and social economic accountability of the blossoming bio-technology industry. I consult in Tanzania to the livestock industry. They have 13 million cattle and they have many, many serious disease problems. It would be wonderful if we could provide genetically engineered vaccines to protect these animals so that we can feed the people first. Unfortunately, Tanzania might be tempted, like Botswanaland, under the auspices of the British Overseas Development Corporation, to raise livestock for export as a cash crop to have foreign exchange, but we should not forget the wisdom of Mahatma Gandhi, who said, 'The cattle of the rich steal the bread of the poor'. We face incredible agro-chemical and industrial pollution and this is one area where the pharmaceutical and petro-chemical industrial complex now profits at both ends. They manufacture chemicals that poison the food chain and then profit from treating us once we get sick. This is not an unholy alliance, but it is the way things have evolved. It is very convenient.

One of the most toxic natural products on the planet is mother's milk, because of our position in the food chain. So it is intriguing how Government also plays in with its regulations and pandering to private interest to maintain the status quo which really does need to be broken. We need an environmental holistic medicine and a more healthful agriculture before we can be well, and this will certainly liberate many animals from the research laboratories. Babies are being born with a variety of genetic defects, metabolic problems and so on. They are not, of course, all related to these environmental factors, but I will deliberate on this in a moment.

Cancer is certainly linked with a lot of our agro-chemical and industrial pollutants; also with a high incidence of meat consumption. High meat and fat intake is linked with various forms of cancer, greater incidence of ovarian and breast cancer in females and, interestingly, a high incidence of osteoporosis. So, basically, using meat as a staple in one's diet is not wise for health reasons, as well as for all the other reasons I have alluded to so far. We cannot protect the foetus from these outside factors, so the next approach, looking further down the line with a future-scope, we could have a scenario where we have a completely uninhabitable environment and we use genetic engineering and bio-technology to genetically engineer us to adapt to such a pathogenic environment. This possibility is not beyond question.

They are now genetically engineering mice, especially at the frontiers of bio-technology, to look at ways to boost the immune system. There are many factors weakening our immune systems – increased lead in the water and atmosphere, increasing ultra violet radiation, many of the pesticides, the heavy metals, cadmium in our water. All these factors weaken our immune systems. So, using this technology to make us tougher is not really the best solution. Profitable – yes. The same goes for farm animals developing genetically engineered vaccines to make them adapt to intensive factory-farming methods. They will still suffer the stresses of those conditions, though they may not succumb to specific diseases. The companies profit from these new products, but the farmers really do not, because it is more capital input, and the farm animals do not. So we should see the writing on the wall.

There is this image of a world without disease. The hope of a world without disease in the genetic age is here. But, let me point out, as the corporate executives rush to develop new animal models of human disease, we must keep this in mind. Some of these genes are inherited, but others can be transformed. There are many environmental factors that can trigger our genes to behave in wild ways which genetic engineering is not going to stop. What are they doing to animals, creating birth defects through genetic engineering? Remember, in the United States, as has been pointed out, rodents – rats and mice – are not protected under the Animal Welfare Act. We are trying to work to have them included and have a greater emphasis placed upon this whole transgenic area.

They have produced a mouse that is blind and has brain

disorders and another that is a wobbler mouse; it has a neurological defect which it has inherited through selected breeding by man, and with a little genetic manipulation it can be 'healed', so they call this success. But the animal strains are already ill in the first place. There is one strain of genetically engineered mice that has diabetes. The human insulin gene was inserted into their germ line, and they did not develop diabetes, but soon they died from producing too much insulin, and this is one of the problems. We cannot regulate these genes effectively yet in animals or human beings.

Now one of the first 'successes' was the development of a giant mouse. This contains a human growth gene. So, they thought, 'Well, if we can do this to mice, let's do it to pigs so that we can have super faster-growing pigs, the dream of ever more pork. Perhaps, if they eat less, we might have more meat for nothing.' And some of the first results of this from the US Department of Agriculture were pigs which did not grow twice as big, twice as fast: they were smaller than normal, they were crippled and they suffered from a complex growth disorder. They were very prone to pneumonia because their immune systems were weakened and they developed gastric ulcers. It was a complete wreck of a mess, but the research is continuing. One little gene is introduced and the whole house can be upset as a consequence. The pig could not see very well either because of the abnormal growth of the skull.

We now have transgenic sheep in various places. They are trying to change the growth of the fleece and possibly produce whole new chemicals. We have bovine growth hormone now which has been used to inject into cattle to make them grow faster and produce more milk. We have transgenic poultry which have greater resistance to certain diseases, but as I said earlier, this technology is being applied to existing systems of intensive livestock and poultry production which it really should not be – for animal welfare reasons, for economic reasons, for environmental reasons and for consumer health reasons. In the large broiler sheds there is much stress; this is true also of the swine-confinement operation and the calf-confinement system.

Well, look at some of the words the industry is using. *Genetic Engineering News*: 'UK scientists succeed in transformation of animals into factories for protein production.' There is much hoopla that the next wave of animal agriculture will be having farm animals that produce in their milk or serum a specific pharmaceutical that will be separated out and given to people who have various genetic defects so that they themselves do not produce these essential elements in their bodies, such as Factor 9 for haemophiliacs.

One small group of sheep from Scotland which had been made transgenic are producing Factor 9 and some other compounds in their milk now. So there are many different areas in which farm animals could be used, and the idea is that we are going to have the new harvest of genetically engineered species. There are many ethical questions here; there are many economic questions too. Is this the best way to develop new pharmaceuticals? We have genetically engineered bacteria that are producing insulin for us. It might be more efficient to use bacteria and other organisms, including plants, to produce these pharmaceuticals for human use rather than relying on farm animals which, in the process of being used to develop these new animal machines, frequently undergo much suffering because the genes do not operate in the right way.

Moving swiftly now, there is great interest here on the part of venture capitalists in bio-technology. It might be the future hope. I have reviewed the issue of animal patenting, and you know that it is on its way. I hope that GATT will not accept the patenting of animals in the next round of talks.

The first animal to be patented in the United States was developed by Harvard University: a little mouse that had its gene spliced with certain human genes which make it very susceptible to breast cancer. Who owns the patent on this little mouse? One of the world's largest manufacturers of carcinogenic chemicals. The idea is that they could profit at both ends. Find ways of screening carcinogens, treating women when they have breast cancer, in part as a consequence of some of these hazarduous chemicals that are being used in agriculture and industry. The whole genetic structure of cattle and other farm animal species might soon be looked at for future manipulation. A survey done a number of years ago now, in 1987, in the United States, indicated that 35 per cent of people believed that we should not interfere or tamper with nature. For an uninformed public this is an interesting gut reaction.

Now I did not say it is an emotional reaction, I said it is a gut reaction. I think there is a lot of wisdom at this level, an intuitive wisdom that when we feel that something is not quite right, we should raise an awful lot of questions. But the bio-technology industry with its strong alliance with Government, which together represent the rising technocracy of today, will have no such debate. There are erroneous public fears of giant animals running around – like a huge calf, for example, running out of the lab. In fact giant fish have been created with, again, inserted human growth genes or by doubling up their own growth genes. There are possible risks of accidental release into the environment from compounds where these fish are being raised for human consumption.

So, to summarise, we have power over the atoms of matter and now power over the genes of life. If we decide to use this power for better or for good it is up to us to make the wise decisions. We can use it for good or for evil, for war or for healing. There are alternatives to animals for developing new pharmaceuticals. Rape seed, for example, is a commodity oil seed, growing primarily in Europe. It has been genetically engineered to produce high value speciality oil. So we do not need oil from whales any more.

Plant genetic systems create plants that produce peptides, and essential chemicals used to heal human beings. We can genetically engineer algae and other micro-organisms to provide a food source for human beings and for animals. We can engineer bacteria to help purify water that is so seriously contaminated today, and they can also be used to leach out trace minerals and precious metals from soils and alluvium. So there is a good side to them.

There is much pollution of water, and the appropriate use of genetically engineered bacteria in water purification could greatly help. Flasks are filled with microbes that have been genetically engineered to produce interferon: a compound that could prove useful in checking some cancers, AIDS and other diseases.

With careful use, and a sense of reverence, it will be all right. It was said in the 1950s that we are rapidly reaching the point in our biological evolution where we will have one final choice and that will be between suicide or adoration. So, as we take the stepping stones across animal rights towards a unified vision of a respect and reverence for all creation as creative participants in the earth process, we might be able to pull ourselves away from the brink of the most terrible accident in creation, which was the emergence of the human species. As Andrew Linzey says, 'to be part of the world, to be its masters, we must serve it', and this attitude of service towards the creative process is the way in which the humane movement, animal protection and environmental movements are converging rapidly today.

As we exercise our dominion for the integrity and future creation it is all in our hands; nobody is going to save us. We could produce cows that are mindless biological machines. Let us rail against this. It is anti respect and reverence for all life.

We should question BST. This is a whole complex issue, but many of the new developments in bio-technology need to have thorough social and economic studies done before they are applied. Because, for example, we are losing many farmers to some of these agribusiness developments. In the last ten years we have lost 450,000 farmers in the United States and we are losing 4 to 5 billion tons of topsoil a year. Things have to change. We need a humane sustainable agriculture with less disease because animals are treated more humanely. We can use this technology to enhance the health of farm animals, but we must reduce their numbers because, worldwide, the deserts are growing and the world is heating up.

So, to conclude, a little flip back to the idea of our relationship to creation. In Genesis 1:26 it says that we have dominion over all of creation. The original meaning of dominion comes from the Hebrew word. It means to come down to, to have communion with; it does not mean to dominate over. Thomas Berry, one of the leading theologians of the creation-centred movement to save the planet today, says that we must rise to embrace a communion of subjects. We must cease objectifying the world, with the kind of duality that Jonathon Porritt talked about. We must have a communion with the subjective – reverence, in other words, with all life. We must recognise the fearful symmetry of every being of creation, an aspect of divine revelation, and the sacred unity of the earth itself for us to cherish and revere. If we do, we may fight back against the increasing suffering of humanity and the dying of the planet and see the world in a new way through the eye of compassion and humility.

14. Wild Animal Welfare

James Kirkwood

The subject of my paper is intervention on behalf of the welfare of free-living wild animals: if, to what extent, and how it should be done. Some have advocated that we should leave wild animals entirely alone, but others have presented the view that we have a responsibility for their stewardship. History gives little cause for confidence that in future man will be able to avoid harming wild animals completely. Oil spills and other environmental insults are, for example, likely to be a feature of life for some time to come.

When wildlife incidents occur, such as the 1988 seal morbillivirus disease outbreak in the North Sea, or the oiling of sea otters in the spill from the Exxon Valdez in Alaska in 1988, or whenever sick or injured wild animals are found, should we intervene or not? My view is that, at the least, the causes of disease and mortality in wild animals should be investigated because otherwise we will not know if man is a factor or not. Furthermore, I consider that intervention is appropriate in some cases.

I will discuss some of the ways in which man compromises, or has compromised, the welfare of wild animals, provide examples of the kinds of interventions that have been made, and finally illustrate the state of wild animal medicine with a few examples that reflect my own interests.

Man's impact on biodiversity

There is no need for me to review here the impact of man on the environment and on populations of wild animals. We are all aware of the extensive literature documenting threatened and endangered species. During the last two years the balance of public opinion seems to have swung from a scepticism that a real and serious threat to the environment exists, to a clear awareness of the need for active measures to protect it. There is wide support for the aims of species and habitat conservation even if priorities, methods and level of investment for them remain in debate.

Reduction in biodiversity is an important issue, but it is not the subject of this meeting. Unless the factors leading to it cause individual suffering, extinction is not a welfare problem. Active conservation measures have probably already saved many wild populations, and far more remain dependent on them. Our control of the fate of these populations brings with it some responsibility for the welfare of the individuals of which they are comprised.

Man's impact on the welfare of wild animals

Man and his domestic species are in competition with other species for resources, for example for food and space. This conflict has not only had a detrimental effect on the size of many wild animal populations but also, sometimes, on the quality of their lives. There are many ways in which man's activities can compromise the welfare of wild animals.

For example, suffering can be caused by injury or deprivation of food or shelter resulting from disturbance, damage or destruction of habitat. Such habitat insults can be severe; as when land is developed for farming, mining or housing, or when the environment is contaminated with toxins (Environmental Panel of the Advisory Committee on Pesticides, 1989), or with oil spills (Gullett, 1987), or when exotic species which prey on, or compete with, indigenous fauna are introduced (e.g. Garner & O'Brien, 1988; Johnson & Stattersfield, 1990). Even mild insults, such as unintentional disturbance at feeding or breeding sites, may compromise the welfare of the disturbed animals or their nestlings.

Diseases can cause severe suffering. Some, for example myxomatosis (Ross, 1982), have been introduced intentionally as biological control measures, but many others have been spread unintentionally to new host species or populations with translocated animals. For example, rinderpest was introduced to Africa in this way at the end of the last century and caused a massive pandemic (Pastoret et al, 1988); the greater liver fluke *Fascioloides magna* was introduced to the wild deer population in Italy with imported wapiti *Cervus elaphus* from North America; and rabies has become endemic in the raccoon population of the Eastern United States following the release of an infected animal in the area (Anthony et al, 1990). Some diseases can spread from man to wild animals. Many primates are susceptible to measles, and there has been concern that this disease could be, and perhaps has been, transmitted to Mountain gorillas by tourists (Sholley, 1989).

Man can also cause suffering in wild animals by the use of inhumane methods to control, kill or trap those species regarded as pests, threats, competitors or food (Nevill, 1985; Meehan, 1985).

It is also worth mentioning that some conservation measures and treatment and rehabilitation of wildlife casualties may have a welfare cost. Even when successful, treatment and rehabilitation of wild animal casualties is unlikely to be accomplished without any fear, pain or stress (British Wildlife Rehabilitation Council, 1989), and the same applies to some conservation measures such as translocations and reintroductions.

Protection of the welfare of wild animals

There is a considerable body of legislation which exists to protect the welfare of wild animals, and valuable reviews on this aspect of British law have been provided by Cooper (1987) and Sandys-Winsch (1984). This legislation is largely concerned with preventing disturbance and harm to wild animals and in regulating methods used in the control and culling of pest and other species. Legislation and codes of conduct also exist to protect the welfare of wild animals in field research programmes (Cooper, 1987; Williams, 1988).

It is generally accepted that we should take care to minimise or prevent the risk of compromising the welfare of free-living wild animals by our own activities. However, the rigour with which this principle is applied varies. Regulations for shipping oil have been tightened but the shipping of oil, which will always pose a risk to the well-being of marine animals, is permitted. Efforts are made to control pests humanely, but pest control is not outlawed on the grounds that available methods do not guarantee complete lack of suffering. Where such lines are drawn, balancing human against wild animal interests, varies between cultures and with time.

Intervention for wild animal welfare

Opinions differ about the degree of responsibility we have, beyond existing legislation, for the welfare of free-living wild animals and for the degree to which we should intervene to protect or improve their welfare. There has been considerable debate about these issues recently (e.g. Cooper, 1989; Howard, 1989; British Wildlife Rehabilitation Council, 1989). Two factors have perhaps been important in precipitating this debate: first the growing concern about the welfare consequences of man's impact on the environment and, second, the development of techniques of wild animal health assessment, management and medicine to the stage at which we now have the capacity to intervene to improve the welfare of individual free-living animals in some circumstances.

Several factors influence attitudes to our responsibility or involvement in the welfare of free-living animals. These include:

(a) the extent to which man is perceived to be responsible for the harm (e.g. oil-spillage *versus* cold-stress),
(b) the extent to which the animals are under our stewardship (e.g. if they have been translocated for conservation purposes *versus* if they are entirely independent),
(c) the popularity of the animal (e.g. seal *versus* rat), this is an illogical but potent factor.
(d) the conservation status of the animal (e.g. endangered *versus* common) and,
(e) the severity of the welfare problem (e.g. severe chronic disease *versus* disturbance at the nest site).

Some take the view that we should not interfere in the welfare of wild animals at all, others that veterinary surgeons should be prepared to treat injured or sick wild animals brought to them (and that euthanasia is unacceptable under almost any circumstances). Most would probably agree that when wild animals are harmed by man's very recent (in evolutionary terms) changes to the environment (such as oil-spills, power-lines, roads, and environmental contamination) there is a reasonable case, on welfare grounds, to intervene.

Positions also vary as to whether, or to what extent, we should intervene in cases where the welfare of free-living wild animals is compromised by factors other than man. Wild animals have always fought their own battles with competitors, with parasites and other infectious agents, and with the rigours of the environment, and they are as they are anatomically, physiologically, immunologically and behaviourally, precisely because of this. Careful consideration is warranted before interfering with natural selection and before taking sides to influence the outcome of these struggles.

If habitats are artificially maintained or created in order to encourage certain species (e.g. the maintenance of heathland for nightjars or the digging of pools for wading birds), then it is not a great step further to provide a health service for the animals of the resulting populations. In taking on a responsibility for stewardship of the environment and actively controlling it we influence the fate of the wild animals dependent on that environment. It would not be illogical to argue that with this comes a degree of responsibility for the welfare of those animals.

Leaving the issue of our perceived level of responsibility, there are limits as to what intervention is possible for wild animal welfare. These limits are imposed by the technology available, economics, the logistics of working with wild animals, geography, and other factors.

What active measures can be taken for the welfare of wild animals?

In addition to protecting the welfare of wild animals by legislation and codes of conduct which act by preventing or limiting harm caused by man, a variety of active measures involving intervention have been taken which may improve wild animal welfare in the face of specific problems. I will give some examples below.

I have tried to pick examples in which the intervention has been on behalf of the animals for their own sake, and where the intervention has been for welfare rather than conservation reasons, or at least partly so (but often both welfare and conservation are cited as justification for intervention). There are many more situations where wild animals are fed, provided with shelter, or vaccinated as parts of programmes to maintain populations for hunting or to control human or farm animal disease. In these cases, although the prime motive is not to improve wild animal welfare, the measures may nevertheless have this result.

1. Provision of food

In Sweden wild sea eagles have been provided with uncontaminated food in the winter to improve the survival and reduce the pollutant-burdens of young birds (Helander, 1985). Various species of vultures in the Pyrenees have been fed artificially to reduce the risk of poisoning by strychnine (Terrasse, 1985). Friend (1987) has suggested attracting eagles away from the sites of avian cholera (pasteurellosis) outbreaks using road-killed deer. Garden birds are often provided with food in harsh weather conditions. Supplemental feeding can cause population growth beyond the carrying capacity of the habitat, which can lead to crisis, as has been reported in deer in Angel Island, San Francisco Bay (Jessup, 1988).

2. Provision of habitat

The California Department of Fish and Game relocated 800 elk in an attempt to solve a local overpopulation problem. Jessup (1988) described relocation as a 'temporary and expensive exercise'. In Zimbabwe more than 300 wild black rhinos have been translocated to safer areas to protect them from poachers (Kock et al, 1990).

3. Therapy of wildlife diseases in the wild

I am not aware of any published accounts of the treatment-in-the-wild of disease in free-living wild animals on welfare grounds. However, anti-parasitic drugs have been administered to wild animals in baits for research purposes, for example to study the impact of the nematode *Trichostrongylus tennuicollis* on the reproductive performance of the red grouse (Hudson, 1986). Administration of drugs in baits could be used to treat some wildlife diseases, for example mange in foxes.

4. Preventive medicine

There are an increasing number of situations in which free-living wild animals have been vaccinated for their own benefit against virus diseases. For example, mountain gorillas have been vaccinated against measles (Sholley, 1989), and Florida panthers have been vaccinated against rabies (Rupprecht et al, 1990).

Methods of control of disease outbreaks in wild birds have been described by Friend (1987). These include 'shepherding' whooping cranes away from a major avian cholera outbreak (Friend, 1989), and collection and incineration of carcases in outbreaks of duck virus enteritis (Brand, 1987).

5. Euthanasia and culling

In our society, to save sick or injured animals from prolonged pain, stress, or discomfort that cannot be relieved is generally considered to be the reasonable, humane, correct and lawful course of action. Techniques for humane destruction of wildlife casualties have been described by Kock (1987) and Kell (1987), in the UFAW (1978) book on humane killing of animals, a new edition of which is in preparation, and in the International Wildlife Rehabilitation Council/National Wildlife Rehabilitators Association document 'Wildlife rehabilitation minimum standards and accreditation programme'. Deciding whether to euthanase or attempt treatment is often difficult and depends on the nature of the disease or injury and the resources available for treatment. Recognising this difficulty, McKeever (1979) suggested guidelines to assist in the decision in the care of wild owls.

As mentioned above culling has been used to control disease outbreaks in wild animals (Friend, 1987). It has been traditionally used to prevent starvation and stress due to overpopulation in, for example, deer (Staines, 1985; Jessup, 1988).

6. Monitoring wildlife health and disease outbreaks

Health provides an index of welfare. There is a good case for monitoring wildlife health both for this reason and because changes in health status in wild animals can indicate changes in environmental quality. A wide range of techniques are available for wildlife disease monitoring (Friend, 1987; Plowright, 1988; Hunter, 1989). The efforts put into wildlife health monitoring and the way in which this work is organised vary from country to country.

In the United States of America the National Wildlife Health Research Center was established by the Fish and Wildlife Service (FWS) in 1975 with a broad remit. This was to determine the causes and impact of diseases on the wildlife under FWS stewardship, to develop means for preventing these diseases, and to reduce wildlife losses when diseases occur (Friend, 1988). Many other countries also have state agencies for the investigation and monitoring of wildlife diseases.

In Britain, there is no central agency responsible for monitoring wildlife health and disease outbreaks and for maintaining records and disseminating information on this subject. The Ministry of Agriculture Fisheries and Food does investigate wildlife incidents in which death or illness is suspected to be due to pesticide poisoning (Environmental Panel of the Advisory Committee on Pesticides, 1989), and the State Veterinary Investigation Service undertakes some wildlife pathology investigations. In addition to this there are a number of individuals in universities and other research institutes who undertake some wildlife disease work.

There is no shortage of expertise or facilities in Britain but, because of the lack of a coordinating centre, when wildlife disease outbreaks have occurred they have often not been investigated at all or investigations have been incomplete. Without a central agency to organise investigations, standardise methods, arrange special diagnostic tests, maintain records and undertake epidemiological studies on the patterns of wildlife disease, it is unlikely that changes in wild animal health status due to environmental disturbances will be swiftly detected. A step has been taken to improve this situation by the Department of the Environment who have recently awarded a contract to the Department of Veterinary Science of the Institute of Zoology to employ a veterinary surgeon to coordinate investigations of marine mammal strandings around the coasts of England and Wales (Department of the Environment Press Release, 5th July 1990).

7. *Rescue, treatment and rehabilitation of wildlife casualties*

There has been a great increase in interest in the rescue, treatment and rehabilitation of wildlife casualties in many countries of the world. Several veterinary schools in the USA and Canada now run wildlife clinics, so do some zoos, some animal welfare organisations, and an increasing number of private individuals. Facilities and standards of care vary greatly. Policies also differ between these organisations but most do not limit their attention only to those animals made casualties by man (although often the bulk of cases submitted fall into this category e.g. McKeever, 1979; Fix & Barrows, 1990). Most exercise some selection in the species with which they deal and, for economic or other reasons, may not take on very common or pest species.

At the Willowbrook Forest Preserve in Illinois a veterinary surgeon is employed to attend to the health and welfare of the animals in the reserve (Dr Erica Miller, personal communication). Although no veterinary surgeons are employed specifically to provide this kind of service on British nature reserves, injured or sick wild animals found at these locations are sometimes taken for treatment.

There are arguments, in addition to the broader debate about responsibility for wildlife welfare, for and against treatment and rehabilitation of wild animals and I will list some of each, beginning with those against.

(a) Rehabilitation is irrelevant to the conservation of most species.
(b) Rehabilitation may result in the survival of the less-fit and, in the long term, lead to development of less well-adapted strains.
(c) Rehabilitation diverts efforts from habitat and population conservation.

(d) Rehabilitation may lead to suffering. There are several ways in which this could happen, for example: if the animal is not fit enough to survive when released, if the environment into which it is released is unsuitable, if it carries disease which could infect others, or if it displaces another animal to the latter's detriment (British Wildlife Rehabilitation Council, 1989).

The points raised in favour of wildlife rehabilitation include the following.

(a) Individual animals may benefit.
(b) Rehabilitation can play a part in species conservation. Some cases in which rehabilitation has had a direct and significant impact on population sizes are given by Harris (1989). From a purely welfare perspective the conservation impact of rehabilitation is not relevant.
(c) Treatment and rehabilitation of wild animals provides an opportunity to learn about the causes of wildlife diseases and to monitor their incidence, and to develop wild animal husbandry, medicine, and surgery. Knowledge gained in the rehabilitation of common species may be of importance in the conservation of endangered species and in other ways.
(d) Rehabilitation is a subject of public interest and as such can be a focus for the promotion of concern for both welfare and conservation of wild animals.

My own view is that the arguments for wildlife treatment and rehabilitation often outweigh those against. Done well it can contribute to animal welfare, knowledge, and sometimes conservation, but each case should be judged on its own merits.

Recent developments in wildlife medicine and care

Traditionally, veterinary medicine has been largely concerned with the domestic farm and companion species (the name comes from the Latin *veterinae*, meaning cattle or beasts of burden). However, during the last twenty years interest in the veterinary care of both free-living and captive wild animals has increased greatly, and the subject has developed rapidly. The compendia by Fowler (1986) and Wallach and Boever (1983) provide some indication of the state of the subject in the early eighties, and many advances have been made since then. It would be inappropriate to attempt a thorough review here but I will provide some examples of recent developments. The subject is broad and the examples I have chosen are those in which I have a particular interest.

(a) Restraint and anaesthesia

Chemical agents are often necessary to capture and to restrain wild animals for examination and treatment. Great advances have been made in the efficacy and safety of these agents and in equipment for remote injection (Kock, 1987). One notable recent advance has been the development of central alpha 2-adrenergic agonists which reverse the sedative effects of widely used sedative/immobilising drugs (Kock et al, 1989; Klein & Klide, 1989). These reversing agents reduce the duration of the recovery from anaesthesia which is important for free-living animals.

(b) Diagnostic techniques – wild animal haematology

Diagnostic techniques developed for use in man and domestic animals are usually applicable in wild animal medicine but often not directly so. The techniques have to be modified and evaluated. For example, measurement of cellular and chemical components of blood can provide useful diagnostic information in man and the domestic animals. The same is true for wild animals (e.g. Hawkey et al, 1990) but interpretation of the results depends upon knowledge of the normal blood composition and this information is scarce for wild animals.

Recently, computer software has been developed which displays information about the normal blood composition of a very wide range of species of wild mammals, birds, and reptiles (Bennett et al, 1990). This is a useful diagnostic aid for clinicians working with wild animals.

In Britain, and many other countries of the world, many specialised and sophisticated diagnostic techniques are available for investigating infectious, nutritional, and traumatic diseases and there is great potential for extending their use in the investigation and diagnosis of wildlife disease.

(c) Nutrition – milk replacers for neonatal mammals

The nutrition and feeding of wild animals is a vast but very important subject. Many wildlife casualties taken for treatment are young and growing. A particular problem with young mammals is selecting or devising appropriate milk replacers. There are about 4070 species of mammals and milk composition varies widely among them. When no appropriate 'off-the-shelf' milk replacers have been available special formulae have been devised and used with success. For example, a black rhino was recently successfully hand-reared from birth on a specially designed milk (Kirkwood et al, 1990). Problems of formula selection and other aspects of feeding of neonatal wild animals have been discussed by various authors (e.g. Oftedal, 1984; Kirkwood, 1989).

(d) Therapy – prediction of dose-rates for wild animals

A wide range of therapeutic drugs has been developed for use in human and veterinary medicine and many of these are used in wildlife medicine. The appropriate doses and dose frequencies of these drugs for man and domesticated species are based on detailed studies of their disposition kinetics in these species. This information is rarely available for wild animals, nor is it likely that studies of disposition kinetics will ever be possible in more than a few species; thus dosage regimes for most wild animals have to be estimated.

There is no established methodology for making these estimations at present. One approach is to examine patterns of variation in disposition kinetics between species that have been studied, in order to predict disposition kinetics in those that have not. It has been found for example that, between species, there is an inverse relationship between bodyweight and the rate at which the plasma concentrations of some drugs declines following administration (Sawada et al, 1984; Kirkwood & Widdowson, 1989; Kirkwood & Merriam, 1990). Thus, to maintain comparable plasma concentrations these drugs have to be administered more frequently to small animals than to large ones. Practical aspects of dose prediction, based on these considerations, have been addressed by Pokras et al (1990) and Kirkwood (1991b).

The future

I have two suggestions for the future. For both conservation and welfare reasons there is a need to monitor both the population dynamics of wild animals and also their health status. While population dynamics are often monitored closely, health-status and causes of disease and death have been given rather little attention. My first suggestion is, therefore, that efficient systems for wildlife health monitoring are established or bolstered.

Secondly, as I have mentioned, there are many ways in which man can intervene on behalf of the welfare of diseased wild animals at both the population and individual levels. Opinions differ about the value of such intervention but it is my view that it is worthwhile and that support for it will grow. There is a need for an international code on intervention for wildlife welfare to provide guidance on ethics, methods and standards.

References

Anthony, J.A., Childs, J.E., Glass, G.E., Korch, G.W., Ross, L. & Grigor, J.K. (1990) Land use associations and changes in population indices of urban raccoons during a rabies epizootic. *Journal of Wildlife Diseases* **26**, 170-9.

Bennett, P.M., Gascoyne, S.C., Hart, M.G., Kirkwood, J.K. & Hawkey, C.M. (1990) Development of lynx: a unique database for disease diagnosis and health monitoring in wild mammals, birds and reptiles. *Veterinary Record* (in press).

Brand, C.J. (1987) Duck plague. In Friend, M. (ed.) *Field Guide to Wildlife Diseases*. United States Department of the Interior Fish and Wildlife Service, Washington DC. Resource Publication 167, 117-27.

Bredy, J.P. & Botzler, R.G. (1989) The effects of six environmental variables on Pasteurella multocida populations in water. *Journal of Wildlife Diseases* **25**, 232-9.

British Wildlife Rehabilitation Council (1989) *Ethics and Legal Aspects of Treatment and Rehabilitation of Wild Animal Casualties*. BWRC, c/o RSPCA, Horsham.

Cooper, J.E. (1989) Care, cure or conservation developments and dilemmas in wildlife rehabilitation. Harris, S. & Thomas, T. (eds) *Proceedings of the Inaugural Symposium of the British Wildlife Rehabilitation Council*. BWRC, c/o RSPCA, Horsham, pp. 14-23.

Cooper, Margaret E. (1987) *An Introduction to Animal Law*. Academic Press.

Environmental Panel of the Advisory Committee on Pesticides (1989) *Investigations of Suspected Poisoning of Animals by Pesticides in Great Britain 1985-87*. Ministry of Agriculture, Fisheries and Food.

Fix, A.S. & Barrows, S.Z. (1990) Raptors rehabilitated in Iowa during 1986 and 1987: a retrospective study. *Journal of Wildlife Diseases* **26**, 18-21.

Fowler, M.E. (ed.) (1986) *Zoo and Wild Animal Medicine*. Second edition. W.B. Saunders & Co., Philadelphia.

Friend, M. (1987) *Field Guide to Wildlife Diseases*. United States Department of the Interior Fish and Wildlife Service, Washington DC. Resource Publication 167.

Friend, M. (1988) Role of the National Wildlife Health Research Center in diagnosing and managing diseases in wild birds. *Proceedings of the American Association of Zoo Veterinarians* 1988, 1.

Garner, M.G. & O'Brien, P.H. (1988) Wildlife disease status in Australia. *Revue Scientifique et Technique, Office Internationale des Epizooties* 7, 823-41.

Gullet, P.A. (1987) Oil toxicosis. In Friend, M. (ed.) *Field Guide to Wildlife Diseases*. United States Department of the Interior Fish and Wildlife Service, Washington DC. Resource Publication **167**, 191-6.

Harris, S. (1989) The release of wild mammals after treatment: rationale, problems and techniques. In Harris, S. & Thomas, T. (eds) *Proceedings of the Inaugural Symposium of the British Wildlife Rehabilitation Council*. BWRC, c/o RSPCA, Horsham, pp. 94-108.

Hawkey, C.M., Hart, M.G., Bennett, P.M. Gascoyne, S.C. Knight, J.A. & Kirkwood, J.K. (1990) The diagnostic value of platelet counts in mammals. *Veterinary Record* **127**, 18.

Helander, B. (1985) Winter feeding as a management tool for white-tailed sea eagles in Sweden. In Newton, I. & Chancellor, R.D. (eds) *Conservation Studies on Raptors. ICBP Technical Publications* **5**, 421-7.

Howard, W.E. (1989) *Nature's Role in Animal Welfare*. Universities Federation for Animal Welfare, Potters Bar.

Hudson, P.J. (1986) The effect of a parasitic nematode on the breeding production of red grouse. *Journal of Animal Ecology* **55**, 85-92.

Hunter, D.B. (1989) Detection of pathogens: monitoring and screening programmes. In Cooper, J.E. (ed.) *Disease and Threatened Birds. ICBP Technical Publication* **10**, 25-9.

Jessup, D.A. (1988) Relocation of wild ruminants: overview of management considerations. *Proceedings of the American Association of Zoo Veterinarians*, 115-18.

Johnson, T.H. & Stattersfield, A.J. (1990) A global review of island endemic birds. *Ibis* **132**, 167-88.

Kirkwood, J.K. (1989) Artificially rearing wild mammals: rationale and techniques. In Harris, S. & Thomas, T. (eds) *Proceedings of the*

Inaugural Symposium of the British Wildlife Rehabilitation Council. BWRC, c/o RSPCA, Horsham, pp. 47-57.

Kirkwood, J.K. (1991a) Wild mammals. In Beynon, P.H. & Cooper, J.E. (eds) *The BSAVA Manual of Exotic Pets*. 3rd edition. British Small Animal Veterinary Association, c/o British Veterinary Association, London (in press).

Kirkwood, J.K. (1991b) Prescribing for exotic terrestrial vertebrates. In Greenfield, J.R. (ed.) *The Veterinary Formulary*. Pharmaceutical Society of Great Britain (in press).

Kirkwood, J.K. & Merriam, J. (1990) Variation in plasma halflife of gentamicin between species in relation to bodyweight and taxonomy. *Research in Veterinary Science* (in press).

Kirkwood, J.K. & Widdowson, M.-A. (1990) Interspecies variation in the plasma halflife of oxytetracycline in relation to bodyweight. *Research in Veterinary Science* **48**, 180-3.

Kock, M.D., La Grange, M. & Du Toit, R. (1990) Chemical immobilisation of free-ranging black rhinoceros (*Diceros bicornis*) using combinations of etorphine (M99), fentanyl and xylazine. *Journal of Zoo and Wildlife Medicine* **21**, 155-65.

Kock, R.A. (1987) Remote injection systems: science and art. *Veterinary Record* **121**: 76-80.

Kock, R.A., Jago, M.., Gulland, F.M.D. & Lewis, J. (1989) The use of two novel alpha 2 adrenoceptor antagonists, idazoxan and its analogue RX821002A in zoo and wild animals. *Journal of the Association of Veterinary Anaesthetists* **16**, 4-10.

McKeever, K. (1979) *Care and Rehabilitation of Injured Owls*. W.F. Rannie, Lincoln, Ontario.

Meehan, A.P. (1985) Humane control of rodents. In Britt, D.P. (ed.) *Humane Control of Land Mammals and Birds*. Universities Federation for Animal Welfare, Potters Bar, pp. 28-36.

Nevill, P. (1985) Humane control of moles. In Britt, D.P. (ed.) *Humane Control of Land Mammals and Birds*. Universities Federation for Animal Welfare, Potters Bar, pp. 113-17.

Oftedal, O.T. (1984) Milk composition, milk yield and energy output at peak lactation: a comparative review. *Symposia of the Zoological Society of London* **51**, 33-85.

Pastoret, P.-P., Thirty, E., Brochier, B., Schwers, A., Thomas I. & Dubuisson, J. (1988) Diseases of wild animals transmissible to domestic animals. *Revue Scientifique et Technique, Office Internationale des Epizooties* 7, 705-36.

Plowright, W. (1988) Research on wildlife diseases: is a reappraisal necessary? *Revue Scientifique et Technique, Office Internationale des Epizooties*, **7**, 783-95.

Pokras, M.A., Karas, A.M., Kirkwood, J.K. & Sedgwick, C.J. (1990) An introduction to allometric scaling and its uses in raptor medicine. *Proceedings of the Symposium on Veterinary Care of Wild and Domestic Raptors*, University of Minnesota, 1988 (in press).

Ross, J. (1982) Myxomatosis: the natural evolution of the disease. *Symposia of the Zoological Society of London* **50**, 77-95.

Rupprecht, C.E., Nuss, J. & Roelke, M. (1990) Vaccination of Florida panthers (*Felis concolor*) against rabies. *Abstracts of the VIth International Conference on Wildlife Diseases, Berlin*. 54.

Sandys-Winsch, G. (1984) *Animal Law*, Shaw & Sons Ltd, London.

Sawada, Y., Hanano, M., Sugiyamam, Y. & Iga, T. (1984) Prediction of the disposition of beta-lactam antibiotics in humans from pharmacokinetic parameters in animals. *Journal of Pharmacokinetics and Biopharmaceutics* **12**, 241-61.

Sholley, C.R. (1989) Mountain gorilla update. *Oryx* **23**, 57-8.

Staines, B.W. (1985) Humane control of deer in rural areas. In Britt, D.P. (ed.) *Humane Control of Land Mammals and Birds*. Universities Federation of Animal Welfare, Potters Bar, pp. 105-10.

Terrasse, J.-F. (1985) The effects of artificial feeding on Griffon, Bearded and Egyptian vultures in the Pyrenees. In Newton, I. & Chancellor, R.D. (eds) *Conservation of Raptors. ICBP Technical Publications* **5**, 429-30.

Wallach, J.D. & Boever, W.J. (1983) *Diseases of Exotic Animals*. W.B. Saunders Co., Philadelphia.

Williams, E.S. (1988) Animal welfare and the study of free-ranging wildlife. *Proceedings of the American Association of Zoo Veterinarians* 1988, xv-xvi.

15. Science and Animal Welfare: A Summary

Anthony Suckling

I have been asked to sum up the contributions in this section. A difficult task – there has been much to think about in all the talks. All the speakers are experts in their particular subjects and it would be presumptuous of me to try to summarise what has been said.

Instead, I confine myself to a few points that struck me particularly forcibly. We have heard something about environmental issues but somewhat more about animal welfare; understandably in view of the affiliations of most of us. What about the linkage between the two, the purpose of this conference?

Well, I think I understand the basis for the list of conflicts between welfare and conservation and the environment given by Professor Broom, but, if he will forgive me for saying so, I felt they were, while real, a little contrived. We must also be aware of the environmental problems of high stocking rates and overgrazing, which are also in themselves welfare problems.

What struck me more was that animal welfare and concern for the environment are both part of the wider notion of an improved quality of life for all species; a sense of caring for the environment and everything in it. I was struck, too, by the suggestion of the very great potential power of a combination of the various societies and organisations involved in these two concerns. Concerted co-operative action appears to have an important future in promoting the view of an improved quality of life for all species; and that of course includes an improvement in the quality of life for chimpanzees whose plight was so eloquently described by Dr Goodall. It is so good to hear about progress in achieving a better deal for these animals.

The section has been entitled 'Scientific Advances in the Understanding of Animal Welfare and the Environment'. The last two talks illustrated vividly how science has impacted on animal welfare and the environment, one perhaps badly, as described by Dr Fox, and one with more benefit to individual animals and groups of animals by Dr Kirkwood. The positive approach to wildlife health and rehabilitation motivated by welfare aims, carefully and sensitively handled, will I am sure have an important role for many years to come. It is truly an area in which science is working in the service of animals.

But of course there are always problems – and therefore an argument for and against – which science has to try to help solve. Now science is essentially a practical discipline. A scientist often works by defining a problem, constructing a hypothesis to test, carrying out research to provide objective results pertinent to the hypothesis and then deciding whether or not the hypothesis was correct and whether or not a solution to the original problem can be found. From this practical standpoint it is difficult for me personally to see how we proceed from the philosophical position that we must stop using animals *now*.

How, practically, could we do that?

Practically, it is extremely unlikely that in the next two years, five years, twenty years, or even durng our lifetimes, that objective can be reached. In the meantime the world continues to use animals. Now, today and tomorrow, I see science best serving the animals and the environment by dealing with achievable objectives in reducing use and improving welfare. We must have objectives and they must be achievable.

One end product may be to achieve new legislation, as outlined by Professor Broom. Fine – but with legislation, enforcement is always a problem. It is no good having laws if they are not respected, obeyed and enforced.

So for me, as mentioned by several speakers, *education* is the absolute key to the future. Those of us who are scientists working for animal welfare must try to educate others, inside and outside science, to promote a more caring personal approach – individual personal responsibility, individual personal sensitivity and individual personal compassion. Only when *those* aims are achieved over a far greater proportion of the population than is now the case, will the cause of animal welfare and care for the environment truly be linked.

16. Can We Preserve Wildlife in an Industrial Society?

Edward Goldsmith

I was campaigning for Parliament for the Green Party in 1974, when it was called the People Party, in Suffolk, where my father had been an MP fifty years before. All my supporters were hippies and they did not cut much ice in this highly conservative area, so I dressed them as Arabs, hired a camel and harangued the farmers, telling them that they were destroying the land in Suffolk and this would eventually be the only means of transport. If they wanted to get their sacks from London to Bury St Edmunds in twenty years they would have to use a camel, so they might as well look at mine. I did not get many votes, I may tell you. I was arrested, on the other hand, by an RSPCA Inspector who approached me and served a writ on me, but I could not understand why, and he said, 'Cruelty to camels'. So I said I was only taking it for a walk, and he said that camels did not like the traffic. I said, 'Nor do I'. He said it was a dumb animal and could do nothing about it. I said that I had been complaining for thirty years and a fat lot of good it had done me. I still have the writ in a scrap book somewhere.

To get down to serious things, I think it was Lord Zuckerman some twenty years ago who said that wildlife conservation is undoubtedly a good thing but occasionally one must make sacrifices in the interests of society and human welfare. In other words, he thought there was a trade-off between the conservation of wildlife and the satisfaction of human needs. What I would like to say today is that there is no such trade-off. I think it is quite wrong. I think that those policies which are leading to the destruction and, indeed, the annihilation of wildlife in many areas are precisely those same policies which will eventually lead to the decimation of our human population and even, possibly, our extinction. And I am not exaggerating when I say that. I think that we are making this planet uninhabitable both for wildlife and for humans very quickly indeed, at what rate we don't know, but very, very quickly.

In the last forty years the destruction we have brought to this planet is incomparably greater than all the destruction we have brought to it during man's tenancy of the earth, perhaps a couple of million years, depending how you define man. If you go to South East Asia you can see areas that were 70-80 per cent forest and there is now scarcely a tree left. You can see the destruction wherever you go. In the last forty years it has been just incredible. We all know it, and it is almost a waste of time saying it. We have all seen the chemicalisation of our environment: two million tons of chemical waste we dump in our rivers and ground water. The journal of contamination is increasing all the time. I am not talking about the notion of acceptable levels. Very small levels can do a lot of damage, and that can affect the immune system.

You can see that many of the big wildlife disasters are due to stress: animals like the seals in the North Sea or our trees killed by acid rain. They are not only killed by acid rain; there are areas where the trees are dying where the sulphur dioxide pollution is very limited. They are victims of stress. They have been subjected to the chemicalisation of their environment, to all sorts of different pollutants, heavy metals and God knows what, all possibly in very small amounts, which actually reduce their capacity to handle further insults. They are weakened, their resistance is reduced by this chemicalisation. They are living in conditions that are ever less suitable to supporting them, and this is happening to us too. Hence the increase in all sorts of degenerative diseases. You have got to realise how we are rendering this planet uninhabitable just with greater activity; think of Chernobyl. As a result of the accident there, 20 per cent of the agricultural area of the

Ukraine is now highly contaminated. There are 35 million people living in a contaminated environment. Three and a half million people, I am told, are living in an environment which is so highly contaminated that you can write off the next generation. A whole generation. This area is going to be uninhabitable; it is lived in because it is impossible to evacuate the people.

We are making the planet uninhabitable because of erosion and deforestation. This is proceeding at an unbelievable rate. Even in a country like America we could possibly be losing up to 4 billion tons of topsoil per year; 26 billion tons of topsoil are going worldwide. The deforestation, the salinisation of the soil due to large irrigation schemes, etc., means that we are actually losing perhaps 20 million hectares a year – an area bigger than Britain, every year – making this world, of course, highly unsuitable for wildlife and for people, and the world food problem, which is going to become massive, is largely due to this total destruction of the land. Forces which are leading to the destruction are being accentuated all the time. The Food and Agriculture Organisation of the United Nations proposes to increase the impact of our activities on the land still further.

Deforestation I do not have to tell you about. We are meant to be losing something like 20 million hectares of forest per year, again an area the size of Britain. At the rate at which we are going there will be nothing left in twenty years of our main tropical forests. If you assume that there are about 10 million species of animals, plants, reptiles and insect (it could be 30 million, nobody actually knows) and if we are going to lose half of that, because more than half of them live in these forests, we are then losing something like 250,000 species per year; 700 a day. On average, in the next 20 years that will be the average loss.

I do not have to tell you about the ozone layer, and I do not have to tell you the consequences. I am sure you know the report that came out a few months ago on this very subject, showing you that we are going to have a considerable increase in ultraviolet radiation as the ozone layer is eroded. Other forms of wildlife are exposed to ultra-violet radiation, in particular plankton in the sea; and if the plankton go, the basis of a whole food chain of the ocean goes too. It is like killing off the grass and the land here. Also, of course, it affects the nitrogen-fixing bacteria in the rice-paddies in the tropics; if they go then the effect on world food will be absolutely terrible, if you consider the number of people who live off rice and depend on rice for their sustenance. Also, ultra-violet radiation affects our immune system, very badly, to the point where, even if you give people injections or inoculations against specific diseases, they can catch the diseases despite this. You inoculate someone against polio; he gets polio if he is subjected to sufficient ultra-violet radiation. So this is going to turn us all into AIDS victims.

The destruction of forests which will lead to the destruction of most of our wildlife is something which is going to affect us badly too, because most of the serious epidemic diseases which have affected man in the last historic era are diseases that have derived from other animals. If you remember, the plague was a disease of rodents; and if you remember, malaria was a disease of monkeys. So this transfer of pathogens is made more likely from animals whose habitat has been destroyed and who have largely been made extinct, also because we have come in to closer contact with them than we have done before, and because of environmental changes, as in the case of the plague. These are the sources of our most serious diseases, probably including AIDS, which could be a disease of apes or monkeys.

So by destroying nature and wiping out all wildlife we are creating for ourselves a hideous, inevitable epidemic of these very serious diseases, and they are obviously serious because we have had no experience of them. They have moved straight from other wildlife to us.

Well, this brings us to the obvious theme of global warming, which I do not have to tell you about; you have seen the reports. One came out two or three days ago, by 300 scientists working for the United Nations panel on climate change, and they tell us that the situation is dramatic. We know it is, and we are going on doing nothing about it. We know this is going to affect food and health, and if the climate is really, really, destabilised as we are told it is, we are going to get a temperature that we have not seen since life began 3,000 million years ago.

It is going to make much of our land uncultivable, change wind patterns, change rain patterns, make enormous areas uninhabitable, wipe out wildlife and humans. If it goes on long enough it will be only a matter of time before the planet becomes totally uninhabitable to complex forms of life. How long? We do not know: because of all the positive feedback loops which are being slowly identified, but which are still speculative, and are very difficult to model. So the models on which our present prognostics are made are fairly rudimentary, as our climatologists will tell you. And they do not take into account a load of factors including these positive feedbacks, these chain reactions, we may already have started off.

These problems are closely associated. That is why you cannot look at just one by itself. And they are associated because they are all, in my opinion, the symptoms of the inability of our environment to support the present impact of our economic activities. A study done by UNESCO on arid land just shows that everywhere they found that the land could not support the number of cattle already on the land; where there were five cows there should have been two or one. And this is so wherever you look. It is quite evident that our seas cannot take any more pollution. It is evident that the atmosphere cannot take any more CFCs or greenhouse gases. It is perfectly clear that the impact of everything we do to every part of the environment is far greater than it can sustain. So we are condemned, and this degradation can only increase.

The answer here is, quite clearly, that we have to reduce this impact; there is no other possible solution of our activities upon our environment. Now, of course, everybody tells us that technology is going to do the trick because we have been brought up to believe that technology can do almost anything. But this is a total illusion. Technology can solve technological problems, and some of them are very impressive. It can enable us to go to the moon, it can enable us to do all sorts of wonderful things like that. But it does not enable us to repair the destruction done to natural systems like communities, biological organisms; it just does not. No technology is going to bring back a culture which has totally disintegrated, or whose children or young people have become delinquents. There is no technology that is going to bring back a desert that takes between 100 and 10,000 years to create an inch of top soil. There is no technology able to bring back a natural tropical rain forest. It cannot be done, because, as soon as you expose the area to the elements by cutting off the canopy, most of the organisms underneath are killed off by the sun and the storms and everything else. There is no technology that is going to repair the hole in the ozone layer or take the CFCs and the other greenhouse gases out of the atmosphere. Technology is highly exaggerated, and we have exaggerated our faith in it. Of course there is room for technology in reducing the impact of our activities, but even then this is limited.

Let us not suppose that there is a technological solution. The only possible answer to all our problems is massively to reduce the impact of our activities on our environment. I repeat, this is the only real lesson of the whole ecological adventure; the truth is that we cannot continue to support this impact. It cannot be done. To reduce this impact is extremely difficult because we are committed to an enterprise called 'economic development' which systematically increases it. We must not forget what economic development is all about. It is actually systematically transforming our environment. You might as well regard it as a substitute for the world of nature, the product of evolution. A totally different organisation which we can call the world of human artifacts, the world of motorways, reservoirs, factories, housing estates. This is the world that we are systematically substituting for the world of nature on which we must ultimately depend for our survival and our welfare. This is what development is all about and we are totally hooked on it. We cannot get out of it, everything we teach at our universities justifies and rationalises what we are doing. Everybody believes that this is the panacea of all our ills where it is, in fact, the cause of all our problems and can only lead to the annihilation of our species in a matter of decades, and of this I am perfectly certain.

How do we get out of it? You must realise that in the old days for millions of years we lived in small communities and slowly, as we have developed, these communities have disintegrated and our society has been atomised. We have organised it into totally different social groupings which are, in fact, corporations or institutions of one sort or another. And these corporations are very different from our original communities; they are above all single-purpose organisations. They have one goal, to maximise their profit to sustain business. Their job is a purely economic job, and if they are going to stay in business in a highly competitive world they have to subordinate totally all social, ecological, moral and spiritual considerations to the overall goal of maximising the return on capital and keeping in business. Business is business; business comes first and nothing else matters.

You can see what happens when you adopt that philosophy in just one simple field, that of farming. I lived in Cornwall for 17 years and only left last year. There you can see that no living thing that interferes in any way with farming efficiency is allowed to survive. The fox has to go because it kills the chickens, the ravens because they pick out the eyes of lambs, the herons because they eat the trout on the trout farm, the badgers because they transmit bovine tuberculosis, the moles because they interfere with ploughing: all of them have to go. Anything that interferes with economic efficiency has had it. Nothing is allowed to survive. Nothing that can be sold is allowed to survive. No tropical forest is allowed to survive because trees can be sold for timber, or the land used for agriculture, or you can build reservoirs on it, or it can be used for mining. Nothing that can be translated into cash is allowed to survive under this regime. Quite clearly this is not tolerable. At the last meeting in London on the ozone layer, Dupont and ICI lobbied to prevent governments from taking the necessary decisions to protect the ozone layer. They lobbied them, and quite successfully. Is that tolerable? The answer is, it is not.

It is evident to me that we need very considerable changes if we are going to survive on this planet. There are no cosmetic changes possible. If I were a bookmaker, I would give 100-1 against the survival of the human species in the next forty years. The truth about it is that if we are going to survive we need massive changes, and I believe that these large corporations have got to be phased out. I really believe it. There is no possibility of survival if all your social, ecological and climatic imperatives are ruthlessly subordinated to this totally absurd short-term petty goal of churning out more washing machines, more refrigerators and more motor cars, which are, in fact, nothing but toys if you think about it. We are destroying the planet in order to produce toys for a lot of people who have been deprived of their normal functions in the sort of normal world that we have lived in, whose functions have been taken over by governments and corporations.

This terrible addiction is leading to the most preposterous

projects which can only destroy wildlife and make our lives less habitable. Take one example, the case of the Lamada Dam being built in India. It is a huge complex of dams, 33 big ones, 37 huge ones, 133 medium ones and 3,000 little ones. A massive complex costing $20 billion. It is quite unnecessary. India has never finished any of the dams it has started. The project will lead to the expulsion from their land of one million peasants, who will then be condemned to living in the slums; it will lead to the destruction of vast areas of valuable forests; of flooding of massive areas of agricultural land. All this should be intolerable, but they are still going ahead. They are going ahead although the Japanese quite recently decided not to put any money into it. The reason is not that it was required but that it has satisfied the requirements of a large number of people. We, the West, want to sell them the equipment, contractors and engineers. The World Bank is financing it and pushing for it. The World Bank needs to lend $25 billion a year, and this is a very difficult thing to do – more and more so as most countries are now largely bankrupt. The state governments want it, because if you spend a large amount of money in your state, you can make an enormous amount of friends. You can see that everybody stands to gain by building a project of this sort. Rather like our Channel Tunnel, a completely lunatic project. We all stand to gain from it except, of course, nature. And of course the tribal, peasant people who live there who are being totally sacrificed. It is not a unique project. There are thousands of them happening at this moment, all for the same reason. We are totally hooked on this enterprise of economic development.

Unfortunately, when we try to solve these problems we are faced with today, even the solutions we propose are development schemes in disguise. The Tropical Forestry Action Plan which Mrs Thatcher gave £100 million to last year is a fraud. It was apparently a plan to save the world's forests; it is not. It is a plan to set up vast industrial plantations of eucalyptus trees to make money for a lot of people, but it is not actually going to save the forests; it actually has the effect of destroying them. It is a development project in disguise pretending to solve a problem. Our plan to solve the world's food problem, the green revolution, has got nothing whatever to do with feeding the Third World, absolutely nothing to do with feeding people. It is a plan to sell agrochemicals and tractors and things of this sort and increase export earnings of these countries in order to develop further.

Even our aid is largely tied aid. People can only buy things that are made here to get the aid, like Westland helicopters. All the aid is just an export subsidy. Big corporations who find they cannot sell their stuff abroad go to the DTI or the ODA and they give them aid on condition that they buy our products, so they manage to sell to the country in queston. We are not trying to solve the problems, we are not in a position to solve the problems. Our governments and industrialists have other priorities. They cannot begin to solve these problems without forgoing all sorts of short-term economic and political advantages which they cannot afford to forgo. So we are in fact caught up in this direction and we cannot break out.

What do we do? How do we solve it? It may well be, of course, that Saddam Hussein will solve it for us. He might be going to, and it is a terrible irony that this pathological killer should actually do what our Government should have done already. It looks as though he is going to put up the price of petrol which is the first thing our Government should have done. We have been told by successive panels of some of the best climatologists that we have got to cut down greenhouse gases by 60 to 80 per cent now. We have done nothing about it whatever. We talk vaguely about stabilising the production of greenhouse gases by the year 2000 or 2005, which is a waste of time.

If Hussein does not solve the problem for us then we simply have to sit down and reconsider all our options. I think all our various political parties have to meet and admit that we are facing an emergency such as we have never faced before. We have to forget our party differences. We really have to get cracking. Industrialists have really got to get involved too, though I very much doubt they will. We have got to say that we need to reconsider all our policies and phase out present economic activities. It is very difficult to cut down the number of cars. It is very difficult if you live in a place like Los Angeles where you depend totally on the car and there is no other form of transport and you live 40 miles away from your work. But it is perfectly possible to create a sort of society where you do not need a car. If you lived in smaller communities and lived closer to your families and worked in your own village and had smaller corporations, you could live without a car. So it is really a question of creating systematically – I am afraid to say, over some period of time – those conditions in which we need less of all those things we are producing which are causing the destruction of our planet. This is something that *can* be done. We did a plan for it in 1972. We are redoing another one next year, but it is so totally obvious that it is almost embarrassing for me to have to say it. But we seem to have lost touch with the obvious things. We are only looking for highly contrived solutions to what are only obvious problems.

There is nothing else, and the only way to get any programme of this sort and to bring politicians and industrialists to heel, is by arousing public opinion, and that is the only tool we seem to have. I cannot think of any other. People have to realise just how serious their plight is, and they do not yet. They are beginning to. In the last year there has been a big change, but they still do not realise how serious the situation is. My feeling is that if most people in this country realised what little future their children have in this rapidly degrading world, they would co-operate in the sort of plan we need to bring about fundamental change. Such a plan needs to be implemented and I regard it as criminally irresponsible if governments continue to ignore it as they have done so far.

17. The Political Agenda (1)

Bryan Gould MP

I think most people recognise that the environment has moved to the top of the political agenda in a way that could not easily have been foreseen, perhaps even ten or twenty years ago. I am happy to pay tribute to those like Edward Goldsmith, and others, who have made such a powerful contribution to the growing awareness of the damage we are currently doing to our own planet and who have insisted so effectively that politicians should respond to that awareness.

What I am concerned to talk about, however, is the link which this conference has tried to establish between the questions of animal welfare and those wider concerns we have about the environment that we live in. I think it was Einstein who defined the environment as 'everything that is not me'. That is somewhat wide of the definition but it does give us the key. It opens up to us the notion that when we are concerned about the environment, it is not just some global concept of the future of the planet; it is everything beyond our own immediate demands upon that eco-system. Indeed it could be argued that concern for animal welfare was perhaps one of the earliest manifestations of a concern for the environment in quite that sense. The concern for that welfare in many ways pre-dates the current anxiety about environmental issues and in some senses of course it was a manifestation of a somewhat different concern.

What is interesting about the conference, and about the two issues, is the way in which a concern for animal welfare, which began as a rather specific problem-oriented concern, has now moved along an agenda so it has now been subsumed to a large degree in that much wider concern in which we all now share. I believe that the origins of the concern for animal welfare were primarily to do with the recognition that the relationship between humankind and animals is essentially unequal and exploitative. There is very little we can do about that in one sense, in that humankind is powerful; it is in control of its environment, it is able to dominate other species, it turns to other species for exploitation of the products they can produce. All aspects of that relationship mean, as I say, that the relationship is fundamentally very difficult to put on an equal footing.

Those who have been concerned historically with animal welfare have nevertheless tried to accept that that is the nature of the relationship, but to ensure that within it proper respect is paid to the welfare of animals; that cruelty is prohibited, that the true position of animals in the natural society is recognised and that there is a proper expression of our own humanity towards other species. In other words, our concern is not to do with the welfare of animals as viewed as it were from the animal's viewpoint; it is also an expression of our own concern that humankind should behave properly towards other species.

All that that has meant, I believe, is that the emphasis in the past on animal welfare has been directed at what we might call individual responsibility. It has been concerned with that specific relationship between man on the one hand, as owner or farmer or scientist, and animals on the other, as pets or farm animals or laboratory animals. It has been a specific relationship; one might say a closed relationship. It has been a concern with how man treats an animal in a particular situation. For that purpose, a great deal of effort has been made by voluntary organisations to establish a higher level of behaviour and a better system of standards, so that that relationship is properly evaluated, monitored and regulated. Government has played its part in establishing those standards; in looking at the nature of that relationship, in enforcing and monitoring and regulating the standards where appropriate.

Procedures we should concern ourselves with are, first, a change from a specific, individually determined, closed relationship into one with much wider social implications; secondly, a range of new issues which regulate the way in which we impact on other species – some of the issues that Edward Goldsmith rightly drew our attention to. Let me be specific about some of the changes which I believe have now occurred. The social relationship between man and animals (I suppose most obviously characterised by the relationship between the owner and the pet) is rightly one of the main preoccupations of the RSPCA and one of the most obvious manifestations of the difficulties which man has in dealings with other species. It was, as I say, an individual relationship which could be regulated by imposing on the individual an obligation to desist from cruelty and a sanction if that obligation was not met. The pattern of that social relationship has in fact now begun to change, indeed has already changed.

Greater affluence and greater mobility have led to a greater readiness, perhaps a more casual readiness, for that sort of social relationship between owner and pet to develop. I believe that it is now possible for people without much thought to acquire animals for the purpose of treating them as pets, but to invest very little – in either material or emotional or moral terms – in the relationship. We are very much a quick-disposing society. We are accustomed to throwing away things which we like the look of for a brief period but then tire of, and I think that greater affluence, and greater irresponsibility, have begun to characterise our relationships with our pets.

At the same time the position of animals in our society has begun to change also. As society has become more mobile and fluid (some would say more diverse and less coherent), as it has begun to break down in some respects – particularly in our major cities – so the victims have been not just other humans but, I believe, animals as well. Just as we see a lack of responsibility to others manifested in higher crime rates, greater social disorder, the breakdown of family life, and so on, so all these pressures which have had their impact on human society have, I believe, had a knock-on effect on the position of animals. There is a greater social irresponsibility generally, and animals do not escape the consequences of that.

It is those sorts of changes – that greater irresponsibility, that lessening of social cohesion, that increase in the throwaway attitude – that substantially underlie the current debate about dog registration. Now, by comparison with some of the global issues Edward Goldsmith was talking about, there will be some who will say, 'For heaven's sake, dog registration is hardly a central issue when we're confronted with global destruction.' But I hope to argue that the issues are connected, and that there is a continuum between the concern for this sort of specific issue and the wider issues, and the action that is required to deal with them. I content myself with saying 'at the moment', for if we are to grapple with some of those wider issues we have, in a democracy, to enlist the support of many millions of people whose prime concern with the environment – when they are confronted with that issue – is with their own immediate environment. When they are concerned with environment, they mean litter, decent housing, congestion and public transport, and they also mean the way in which dogs are treated in our society. So there is a link, and I believe that we ought not to run away with the idea, attractive though it may be, that if only Edward Goldsmith were a dictator he could save the planet. In a democracy we have to engage public support by adopting sensible policies to a range of issues beginning with those that are most local, most direct and most specific.

Now, on the question of dog registration which has become a great issue, I believe, for some of the reasons I have described, very few people would now dissent from the fact that we do have a substantial problem. I pay tribute to the excellent work of the RSPCA in bringing home to people, in this allegedly dog-loving society of ours, that we are currently disposing of up to 1,000 dogs per day. The poster was shocking, but necessary, to make people understand that in this throwaway society it is the lives of animals which are largely being thrown away. So there is a problem: the problem of disposing of stray and unwanted dogs, the problem of the fouling of public places by dogs and the health risks which that involves, the concern about attacks on humans and animals by vicious dogs, and the use of dogs for dog fighting. All of these are real issues which have to be dealt with and which are recognised by anybody who spares a moment to consider the matter. The problem we face is that we have, I believe, a government that is not prepared to understand that we have moved beyond the point of individual responsibility for these matters; that what we are now confronting is a social issue – an issue which is social in its causes and its consequences. The individual dog owner, the responsible dog owner is, as we all know, not the problem. The problem is, how does society bring to bear its concern and anxiety about the fate of these animals? How does society intervene in an effective way to make sure that this problem is properly dealt with as a matter of social responsibility? The government has problems dealing with this issue because they are ideologically opposed to the notion that society needs to take responsibility for this, or indeed many other issues.

They do not want to see intervention; they want to say (and they are right to say) that this is a matter of individual responsibility, but they do not want to say that it also involves beyond that some responsibility on the part of the community as a whole. That, I believe, is the dividing line that has separated the proponents of dog registration on the one hand from those who oppose it on the other: a dividing line which, incidentally, does not run on party lines. It is interesting that it was the House of Lords, with a substantial Conservative majority, which produced the decisive vote in favour of dog registration. What I think was interesting about that decision was the extent to which it simply imposed upon the government the requirement to bring forward, in principle, a scheme which would work. The precise way in which it would work, the mechanism for registering ownership, the level at which fees would be set and so on, are left open to the government to decide. But what is established by that amendment to the Environmental Protection Bill is the principle that this is a government responsibility, and that some intervention is required with the resources that are needed to back it up and make it work.

I would like to take the opportunity to call publicly on the government to accept the decision made by the House of Lords and not to resist that amendment when it comes back to the House of Commons. I have some hope that the government will heed that plea, because they now understand that they have lost the argument and, notwithstanding many of the practical problems that might arise in respect of a dog registration scheme, that this is the only way in which society itself can recognise that we are now concerned, not just with that closed and individual relationship between the owner and the pet, but with a social question of how society treats animals in that social relationship.

Similar changes have occurred, I would argue, in the other traditional relationship between man and other species: that is, essentially the commercial relationship – the farming relationship, the relationship which uses animals to produce products which we consume or which uses animals to test products of other types. Now, in other times, the very commercial dependence of the exploiting human on the animal species in a sense provided its own regulation of that relationship. It was clearly against the commercial interests of the farmer, or the producer of a product, to exploit animals or treat them badly in such a way that their product was made less valuable or destroyed. That worked fairly well where the market relationship was a short-span one where the link between those who were supplying the product and those who were consuming it was pretty close; where it was possible for the consumer to judge what it was that he was consuming.

But, of course, in a modern economy other forms of manufacturing process have become so large-scale and so complex that most of us have very little idea when we buy animal products what has actually gone into them. We choose in many cases not to inquire too deeply or too specifically into how animals were actually treated in the course of that process. So the market mechanism, a natural regulation of that commercial relationship, has, I would argue, now largely broken down. The market no longer brings to the consumer that information which the consumer needs to base a judgment on whether approval is to be given or withheld. Again, this is difficult for the present government to accept and understand. It takes the ideological position that the market will always resolve the problem. I believe we can no longer assume that that is the case. Two sorts of government intervention are now required:

1. The government has to make sure that the market works better than it would otherwise do and we can do that by insisting on freedom of information; upon the full disclosure of information about manufacturing and farming processes so that the consumer is able to make a judgment between one process and another, one product and another.

Government action is required to make sure those obligations are imposed and enforced.

2. Governments also have to accept that however well the market can be made to work, it simply will not do enough to establish the standards which, in a modern society, we now expect, of those who have the commercial care of animals. Direct government action and regulation is therefore required. Again, I believe that this in essence, on given practical issues, is a matter which need not necessarily divide the political parties, but it has to be recognised that we do start from somewhat different ideological starting points. I would argue that those on the left of politics, who naturally and traditionally espouse a politics of intervention, find it rather easier to contemplate intervention on this account than those who, in other respects, eschew the whole idea of intervention. Yet, in practical terms, I think governments of all political persuasions increasingly accept the need to intervene in order to establish proper standards.

The Labour Party is clear that we will want to improve those standards. We will want to draw on the work of the Farm Animal Welfare Council. We will want to ensure that those who have the responsibility of dealing commercially with animals are properly licensed. We will want to look at specific agricultural processes such as the keeping of battery hens, compulsory and routine de-beaking and the use of confined accommodation for pigs and other animals. All those aspects we want to look at in order to establish higher standards. We are indeed in the course of producing a substantial paper which will set out the details of the proposals we have in this area. We want to see, for example, a ban on the export of equine live animals. We also want to see much tighter monitoring and enforcement of the rules which have been established on the treatment of animals in laboratories. All of this, I think, is commonplace; a question of political will, putting the resources behind the necessary inspectorates, ensuring that the law is applied.

But there are, of course, other dimensions as well, and one of the reasons Mr Simmonds was invited to speak to us is, I think, that the scope for taking action on the national scale is now limited by the operation of the Common Agricultural Policy and by the prospect of the 1992 single market. We must ensure that the measures which we think are necessary are as far as possible adopted on a Europe-wide scale. In that way we help to disarm the critics, who would say that to adopt higher standards is to impose an unfair burden on our agricultural industry by comparison with that of rival economies. My own view on that point, incidentally, is that we really have to get away from the idea that accepting higher environmental and social and welfare standards is always a handicap. The example of more successful economies is often that by adopting those higher standards they actually acquire, in purely self-interested terms, a competitive advantage; the Germans have shown this in many aspects of industry. We should not be slow to press that argument when it comes to agriculture and the treatment of animals.

But we should also be clear that while the EEC dimension is of great importance to us it should be used as a spur to action rather than as an excuse for inaction. I believe that the British government should always be prepared to go out ahead of Europe-wide standards where we think those are necessary. For example, we would want to see the banning of the close confinement in crates of veal calves, and that I think is a standard which goes beyond standards which are now widely accepted in Europe.

So my argument is that, in both the social and commercial relationship between humankind and animals, the traditional relationship – that which I described as a 'closed' and 'specific' relationship – has widened substantially; it can no longer be regarded as simply a matter of individual responsibility. The individual no longer has the information, or the direct relationship with the animal and the process in which the animal is used, in order to exercise any real control. A role for government is essential.

But of course the changes which we now confront are not just those of the traditional relationships. They are the changes which involve some of those wider concerns referred to by Edward Goldsmith. As we understand more, and as our understanding increases of the damage that we are doing to the environment, it becomes increasingly clear that the damage is not just to that wider content of the environment; it is to individual species of animals as a whole. We can see that clearly, for example, in the direct exploitation of wild animals and the efforts to kill and capture whales. I have a particularly powerful illustration from my home country of New Zealand, where a flightless bird, standing about ten feet tall, called the Moa, was hunted to extinction by the native population about two or three hundred years ago. So the problem is not a new one; it is the understanding we now have of the worldwide scale on which it can occur that is new and important.

Our destruction of other species is not of course always a consequence of direct exploitation. I never fail to think as I drive around the Cotswolds and see the carnage on the roads – the huge numbers of corpses of various animals – that this is a paradigm of the whole relationship we have now developed. No one intends to run over badgers or hedgehogs on the road; it is simply an accident, it is simply a by-product of the modern society that we have created. That illustration of the accidental, casual destruction of animals can of course be multiplied a thousand-fold as the pollution which we create destroys the habitats of so many animals; as the economic developments which we bring about physically removes their habitat. In all these ways we now have to understand that the demands we make on the world and on its ecology are at the expense of other species, for whom we have some moral and practical responsibility.

New technology, against which Edward Goldsmith rightly issued his diatribe, does of course create new opportunities for us; genetic engineering is the latest of the attempts by scientists to interfere with the balance of nature in a way which, I believe, is likely to produce quite unforseeable consequences, which we ought to approach with the very greatest degree of caution. The issues are not simply practical ones but ethical ones as well and, just as we set up a Warnock Committee to look at the question of embryology research and to consider the ethical issues which arose in that context, so I think we ought to set up a similar commission to look at the ethical issues of genetic engineering before we go too far down the road and find that we have created a further crime against the survival of other species and other world societies.

If we are concerned about the environment and animal welfare, I would argue that an important aspect of our concern is that politicians have to be asked hard questions and have to be required to give the hard answers as well. Too often campaigners ask politicians the wrong questions. Let me give you what I believe is the right checklist of questions to ask politicians.

1. Do you accept the evidence that there are major environmental issues which now confront us which require immediate action? In other words, do you accept what I would describe as the 'precautionary principle'; that we stop now, and then undertake the research, rather than undertake the research and then conclude too late that we were doing the wrong thing all along?
2. Do we have a coherent politics which enables us to take that action? Do we have a politics which enables us to intervene, not just for the familiar purposes of social justice or economic efficiency, but, on this occasion, to intervene for the purpose of protecting our own environment and the environment of other species as well?
3. Are we prepared to take decisions in that interest which run counter to the sectional interests, to the political preoccupations, to the electoral considerations to which we are accustomed to responding? In other words, is the Conservative Party, for example, prepared to act against its ideological commitment to the free market? Is the Labour Party prepared to act against its traditional protection of jobs and pay packets for working people in this country?

Those are the questions which I believe politicians have to be asked. And, finally, do politicians understand that, while of course it is valuable to go through an agenda of specific problems with problem-related solutions, the real problem we face is not specific in that sense. It is an overall problem which arises from the general nature of man's activity on this planet, and it is that range of activity which now has to be reconsidered. The significance of animal welfare to all of this is that animal welfare (which is comprehensible and matters to so many people) provides for politicians, and others who want to engage in that wider environment debate – and want to get more public support for the policies that are needed to protect the environment – an opportunity to lead them, as it were, through the gate of concern for animal welfare to an understanding that what matters to other species also matters to us, and that in the end those concerns are indivisible.

18. The Political Agenda (2)

Simon Hughes MP

The bit of my pedigree that you may not be aware of is that I used to prosecute for the RSPCA, and no doubt that gives me a few extra points. The other recollection I have is that I often came to this building in my legal phase (which suggests that I am now in my illegal phase – I did not quite mean that!). I was on the Midlands and Oxford circuit. I am reminded of probably the most frightening moment ever in my legal experience when I was defending what was called a 'four hander', namely four defendants on linked charges, before the late Judge Mynett in the Oxford Crown Court. The other people who were assembled with me as counsel for the defence were considerably older and more eminent. What I had not worked out until two seconds before the case began was that the charges had been drawn up and the indictment prepared in such a way that I had to bat first. So, in about my second year of practice, I was thrown to the judge, the jury and the lions by having to perform first on behalf of everybody and make the whole of the case for the defence for all these people who knew how to do it many times better than I did. The advantage today is that although everybody else is, of course, considerably older than me, I go last and have the benefit of having heard what they have to say.

I want to reflect first on the link between the two words 'political' and 'educational'. It seems to me that one of the fundamental necessities is that people are well educated, and I want briefly to remind us how we in this country still educate very badly. It does not need me to draw attention to that.

I recently attended the British Association for the Advancement of Science conference in Swansea where the President drew attention in his address to the inadequacy of our education system. We send many people out of schools unable to read or write, let alone to understand basic scientific facts. We have recently established that everybody has a broad-base curriculum during their school education. Until recently many have been victims, as I was, of the ludicrous education system which gave options at an early age, so that pupils often failed to take any of the standard science subjects at all. It may be one of my main technical defects that I appear to have escaped biology for all of my educational life. After sixteen we send fewer people to higher education than almost any of our competitor countries. In fact if you look at the figures, we send only about 16 or 18 per cent of our population on to further education. The United States sends 50 per cent; Korea sends more now than we target to do in thirty years' time. So the starting point for a society that achieves the sort of common goals that I guess all of us desire is that we have a well-educated society, and we are very far from having that. The second pre-requisite is that we fund, and continue to fund, those who go on to be academics and researchers because, without that pyramid of excellence and information, we are not going to be able to provide the evidence to advance the arguments to bring about the changes.

Again, I am not going to go into the issues in detail, but we are at the moment about to launch on a period where the encouragement to be a student in higher education is reduced because people will have to take out a loan in order to do so. That, I can assure you, representing an inner city seat, means that at the margins people will opt not to do it. But, in fact, we are grossly under-funding academic pay, teachers' pay and scientific research. The big danger that we are seeing at the same time as we, nationally, corporately, collectively reduce our funding is that funding commitment being taken up by others. And who takes it up? It is taken up by corporate interests at home and abroad. Put aside the fact that over 50 per cent of all scientific research and development in Britain is defence-related, appalling though that figure is. Almost all the rest now is short-term, commissioned industrial research on the basis of contracts from companies who want a job done.

That is not in the interests of animal welfare, because by definition it is about product effectiveness and about competitive prices in an increasingly competitive market.

The third concern I have is that we are about to engage as a nation in a debate about what it is to be a responsible citizen. Citizenship is becoming more important as a concept for teaching; it is taking over from subjects like physics in the curriculum. The big problem about the debate is that it talks about rights and duties but is currently limited to rights and duties of a human being. You must look out not only for the report due from the Commission presided over by the Speaker, of which I am the Liberal Democrat member, but also all the other issues of integration and education of citizenship. We need to work hard to convert the debate into one that actually puts humans into the global environment as a whole and not just humans into the interpersonal relationship within the native state. For me the link between animal welfare and the environment is easy. It is easy because we are all required to act with dignity as a consequence of being human beings. And that dignity is our responsibility towards the animal kingdom as well as ourselves. I was prompted the other day to do something which I should not really have had to do, and it is an admission to tell you that I did it. As a Christian I could be presumed to know my first chapters of Genesis; the same would apply to a Jew. But when we were preparing, as we and the other parties are, our environment white paper for this autumn and we were talking about the philosophical principles section, I thought I had better look again at what the Old Testament gives us as a responsibility towards the animal kingdom. Yes, it says that we shall have supremacy. Yes, it says that we are entrusted with the responsibility. But one should read the words again. It is actually much less specific than I ever thought it was in suggesting that we should have any responsibility that allows us to interfere with the lives and welfare of any creatures other than ourselves. It actually entrusts us with a duty and a superiority, but not with an opportunity to exploit. The two principles then that should govern this debate – and they should be adopted by all civilised human beings – are (1) that it is part of our own dignity and our collective dignity that we ensure the welfare of the animal kingdom, but also (2) that part of our duty is to conserve the resources of which we are stewards, and to conserve the ecological diversity which we inherit. What right have we to leave our children and grandchildren with fewer species than there are now? That is the starting point for the debates, which are now much more prevalent, about protecting individual species and the diversity of the animal kingdom.

Of course, in an age of telecommunications and satellites and the rest, international environmental issues, and specifically animal welfare issues, are much easier to get involved in. Sit at home and watch seals being slaughtered, or the Minke whale being hunted by the Japanese, or traditional wildlife programmes about the White Rhino and the rest and you can easily be converted from a pacifist into an activist, and people are much more interested now in international animals. You will see an increasing percentage of the concerns about animal issues which are not British at all, and that is good. But, of course, it is less good if we respect the right of other countries to do what they want. I delivered recently a long letter to the Japanese Ambassador in London protesting that various practices of Japan concerning the animal kingdom were not worthy of a so-called civilised country. The reply was not altogether surprising. Traditionally, we have taken a very old-fashioned view of political theory: that if something is within the responsibility of another nation state we cannot interfere. All we can do is negotiate agreement, and try to find a collective reason or an international conclusion. But we have to challenge that view. I do not see that national boundaries allow people any longer to say 'I'm sorry, you can't tell us what to do.' Above all, I do not believe that we should preclude our own elected representatives from saying to them, 'I think what you do is disgraceful.' It may sometimes be regarded as colonialist or elitist or judgmental, but there are fundamental principles of violence and non-violence, of perpetuation of species and diversity. On the basis of scientific evidence, there are some campaigns which we, as individual human beings, have a right to expect our Government to become involved in. Of course the problem at United Nations level, or at the truly international level, is that there are very few effective agencies. And although we are making progress within our continent, I urge you to think through how much more progress we need to make at the international level. Yes, there is the United Nations environment programme, but it is still in its infancy and it does not do much on animal issues. Yes, there are individual campaigns, like Survival, Elefriends and the rest, but they are only precedents, seeking to change Government action in all sorts of other ways.

Within the context of Europe, one of my criticisms of British pollution is that, of course, we have been such laggard Europeans that often, instead of leading the way, and realising that Europe can set far better standards than we often do, we assume that if it does it is intervention and if it does not it is no good. If we look at all the European legislation on environmental issues – I am thinking in terms of farm animals, anti-toxic policies, export and import of animals and the rest – you will find that Britain is usually very slow in seeking to find an agreement at the highest level of animal welfare. We are not the leaders in animal welfare issues, and it is all part of a reluctance to give power to Europe. Virginia Bottomley, it may be remembered, when she was Under-Secretary at the Department of the Environment, made it clear last year that she was going to resist European Community proposals, which were, according to her own personal views, not on the basis of a general view, that Brussels was interfering too much. If we believe in regulating trade – for example, export and import – obviously we have to do it at European level, and it is no good our being reserved about it. We have to be there and committed, and if this nation goes on being Little England or Little Britain we are not going to have the standards, whether on air pollution or water pollution.

We are particularly bad in the marine environment. It was we who argued for delay in the implementation of rules on dumping of waste in the sea and for much longer delays affecting the marine environment. It is not good enough, and we ought to be aware of how much we failed.

At the national level, I want to say a few words to disabuse anyone who thinks the system works well. Many, I know, who have long been actively involved in lobbying will be aware how frustrating the system is for obtaining change at national level. Here are a few suggestions about the methodology of winning the political argument for animal welfare.

The first prerequisite, of course, for successful campaigning, is information. Not just for the RSPCA but for the politicians as well. Politicians are in many ways very badly informed, because they are not taken very seriously. This is because unless there is a specific issue which is easy to understand, matters are left to the few.

We spend days every year debating the budget and the state of the economy. We spend three days of the year debating defence. We spend, if we are lucky, a day every year debating the arts. We have no annual space for the state of education or science, the environment or animal welfare issues, and we have no structure for precipitating such a debate. There should, in my view, be a standing commission on education, on science, and on environmental matters. The Royal Commission on Environmental Pollution, which reports annually and produces a scientific analysis of the state comparatively and absolutely of these areas of public life, ought then to precipitate the debate within the relevant sector for questioning. Then it ought to come to Parliament, so that one knows every year that there will be a debate on these things and people can be properly briefed, not suddenly learn, as we do the week before, that there is going to be a debate the following week, with no anticipation, no regular programming, and everybody scurrying round to get something done at short notice. We need to give private MPs, individual MPs, far more opportunity. If Government says no, something does not get through. Private members have twenty balloted spots a year, all of which can be thwarted by procedural issues or be lost for reasons which have nothing whatever to do with those issues. Animal issues have most often come up in Parliament through the interest of individual MPs, not through Government proactive proposals. There have been very few Government proposals. The 1986 Act was the only one of significance in the last decade. First you make it difficult for private individuals to get anything changed, and then when there is a chance and the Government is neutral – as, for example, during the Protection of Badger Setts Bill this year – you actually allow a small minority of people to prevent the issue going through which is to be decided by a general vote. On the committee on which I sat dealing with Tony Banks's Bill on Badger Setts there were only three people in all on both sides opposed to that Bill. The Government was officially neutral, though the Minister was supportive; all the other Tories, including the Minister's PPS, were supportive as was everyone on the Opposition side. It did not go through because, as with every Private Member's vote taken, those three people had a right to block it individually. It takes one person only. There is no chance for a democratic resolution by majority vote. If you have that system, it is a lottery how much you get through, and you get through minimal legislation.

If there is one message I want to pass on, it is that unless we change the structures for changing the rules we are not going to win many of the battles. Now that may be a somewhat negative response to very good campaigns by the RSPCA. I applaud the campaigning. But they are fighting against an antiquated and inhospitable system, to say nothing of all the other things I might be expected to say, as a Liberal Democrat, about how ludicrous it is that half the Parliament is not elected by anybody at all and the other half distorts the views of the electorate, so that you get a government in power for eleven years which has never had the support even of half the British people. Unless you get the representative structures right you will not get the policies right, and you will not get the policies right because the British public – as all opinion polls show – have supported many of the changes in policy terms that have not yet been brought about in animal issues. All opinion polls show, for example, a vast majority against stag-hunting, deer-hunting and fox-hunting. Bills should have gone through a long time ago, and yet what do we have to do? We have to rely on local authorities deciding, for example, to have bans on their land because nothing can be got through Parliament. So, change the system and you will then also change the issue.

Finally, let me identify what I see as being some of the important issues of the nineties in terms of what we should now be seeking to change. There is a massive amount of work to do. Not only is animal welfare still understood only by relatively few (though there is a massive interest), but there are an enormous number of campaigns that we have to win. There is a great amount to do to make sure that farming does not become just more and more commercial and less and less acceptable. I am not just talking about battery cages and factory farming; I am talking about transportation of animals; I am talking about the whole way in which we drive our animal kingdom by the demands of food for humans, at home or abroad. That is an unacceptable and unnecessary reversal of the proper order and it should be changed. There is now heightened awareness about food and food issues; popular tabloids carry food campaigns, one of the easy ways to respond to areas of activity. They are willing to lead with animal welfare issues in the context of farming. But I doubt whether we will see many changes unless we have a much more effective agency at the top than a Government department whose principal role is to defend the industry and not to defend the animals in it.

Secondly, we still have to tighten controls on live animal export.

Thirdly, we still need to do much more to prevent unnecessary pain and suffering to animals. The 1986 Act has not been effective; I think the figures are that there has been a 4 per cent reduction in experiments carried out as a result of that legislation. Many of us predicted – I voted against it on the second reading – that it would not be effective. We need clearer principles about how much pain we are prepared to allow in the school lab as well as in the research labs of our major companies.

Fourthly, we still have a lot of work to do, and legislation to change, in relation to the fur trade and the manufacture of traps. It is extraordinary how we go on allowing them to be used so often in this country.

Fifthly, and it is an area I just touched on, there are various forms of hunting which I think as a civilised country we should have dealt with long ago. Still on the national agenda, we have hardly begun to go through the various different forms of hunting that need work.

Sixthly, we need to prohibit generally the use of snares; they are still regarded as a necessary part of a country person's activities. I do not accept that using devices that cause pain is ever necessary.

Seventhly, we have a real battle on to protect the habitat of this country; to protect it against the developers – especially in the South East – and protect it against all those who are negligent. If we are going to change our farming policies to reduce the amount of intensive farming, we have the chance to be ruthless about making sure that people understand the consequences of destroying hedgerows, wetlands and the rest.

We need to make sure that there is a body informing the public of these things, co-ordinating the issues to present them to the public in an effective way. We need to make sure that we do not just get an outline proposal of a response to dog registration but some actual regulations; then we can go on to teach responsible ownership. There is a massive agenda for the nineties. If we want to change the way in which we, as a country, and we, as the world, treat the rest of the creatures who share it with us then we have to provide far more effective structures for educating people, for keeping them informed and then for bringing about those changes. It is as important to do that as it is to campaign ourselves on the substantive points. I hope we will achieve both sets of objectives in the decade ahead.

19. The Role of the European Community

Richard Simmonds MEP

I must begin by declaring my interests. First and foremost, I am a farmer. None of the produce of my farms is supported by the tax-payer, or by the Common Agricultural Policy. I have 6,000 free-range hens and I have thirty horses, none of which will be exported for slaughter. My second declaration of interest is that I am involved with a well-known cosmetics firm. The day I went to work for them was the day they announced that they were stopping testing on animals. And the third interest is that I am involved in a company that has a power station run on methane gas which is sucked out of your rubbish, generating electricity.

I would like to congratulate the RSPCA on two counts. First, in this celebratory year, on the anniversary of the Royal designation, an accolade still absent from those who seek to protect children. And that lack of Royal recognition for the NSPCC says a lot, I think, about our relative attitudes and priorities between man and beast. Secondly, I congratulate the RSPCA on becoming the most influential and effective lobbying organisation in the European Community over the last ten years. The fact is that it has provided the initiative and the manpower and has done the hard work in establishing a twelve-nation lobbying body which is non-party-political. That is a considerable achievement. I should like to pay particular tribute to Edward Seymour Rouse, who was in the driving seat from the start; to Ian Ferguson, his successor; and in particular to David Wilkins who has been a great help to me in the preparation of reports which have resulted in European legislation on farm-animal welfare – the first of its kind ever.

Now there is, of course, a great art to the business of political lobbying, and I can best illustrate it by telling you the story of two bulls, one old and one young, who lived at peace together in a meadow. In the neighbouring meadow lived fifty beautiful Friesian heifers. One day the young bull, noticing a gap in the hedge, raced up to the old bull and said, 'Look, have you seen the gap? Let's race down there and bang a couple of heifers.' And the old bull turned to him and said, 'No, young fellow, we won't do that. We'll walk down leisurely and bang the lot.' And that, actually, is the art of political lobbying: staying on side with everybody, being able to work with people of all party-political opinions, and also with those who do not have a specific party-political affiliation. Members of the European Parliament, if asked what was the single most important issue in the Community today, to judge by the relative size of their postbag on different issues, would have to reply, 'Animal welfare'. Despite flood and famine, war and pestilence, the rise of democracy and the fall of communism, the Euro-voter continues to put pen to paper about perceived and real problems of animals more often than on any other subject. Bulging mailbags about animal issues have always been with us, but they first really exploded in the European Community ten years ago with the campaign to save baby seals.

When the BBC first brought the problems of drought and starvation in the Horn of Africa into our homes, I received some 750 letters from constituents suggesting solutions, and many of those letters were inspired by the great charities. But when the seal campaign really got going, largely orchestrated by the RSCPA and other organisations, I received some 15,000 letters and some 30,000 signatures on petitions from my constituency alone. I wonder what it is in human nature that makes twenty times more people write to elected politicians on the subject of animal suffering than on human suffering? In that seal campaign hundreds of thousands of letters from all over Europe were sent to us urging us to stop the killing of baby seals. The seals themselves were extremely photogenic, lovely little cuddly animals apparently, and the sight of them being killed was particularly horrific. The photographs published in documents sent to us and by the media resulted eventually in donations of thousands of pounds to promote the cause of stopping the killing. The European Parliament, in fact, actually helped to instigate the lobby, and we were instrumental in conceiving and adopting the ban on the import of certain seal skins into EEC countries. We could not have done that without the co-ordinating support given responsibly, diligently and consistently by the RSCPA heading up the inter-parliamentary group in the Parliament.

But today we are so swamped by animal welfare mail generated by some animal welfare organisations (but not the RSPCA) that some campaigns are becoming counter-productive. Eleven years ago, when I first became a Member of the European Parliament, environmental issues were still seen as somewhat cranky. We had not had any proof about the hole in the ozone layer, we were still swimming footloose and fancy-free off contaminated beaches, and we were only vaguely aware of the necessity to clean up water and our air. Let's face it, eleven years ago those issues did not impinge on our daily life as they do today. The animal welfare lobbyists, however, were, unknowingly, years ahead of their time. The decimation of animal species, the destruction of habitats and the general moral indignation of the lobbyists about these things made a substantial impact on the newly elected European politicians. For the first time in several EEC countries questions were asked about, and challenges made to, the commercial exploitation of animals: for instance, by insisting on changes to the battery system for laying hens, an end to the crating of and a more balanced diet for veal calves – something which is already law in this country – and limitations on the use of stalls for pregnant sows.

But, looking back a decade, perhaps we did live in a somewhat simpler world. The urgency of issues like providing a balanced diet for housed goats now seems insignificant compared with the pollution of the atmosphere, with horrendous famines in Africa and all the other macro-environmental issues which confront us daily in the media.

On the other hand, it is sometimes said, those who are kind to animals are usually kind to people as well. Conversely, if we exploit animals for our own gain, will we not in turn do the same to human beings who for one reason or another cannot defend themselves? Then there are, of course, those people who actually prefer animals to people. I can certainly say that I prefer my dog to a number of people I know. And from my mailbag I do know that there are actually people who believe that animals are human. As with many ecological and environmental issues, it is the countries in the developed, Western world who have led the way in animal welfare legislation. But then, perhaps, we can best afford to do so. We were the first to develop some of the most intensive farming systems and now we are starting to back track. But, secondly, we can actually afford now to reduce the intensive nature of some of those systems, whereas some of the poorer, hungrier countries have to go for the system which produces the cheapest food, at least in the short term. Part of my political job is persuading them not to adopt some of the systems that we have adopted over a period of years. The rule of thumb is that the further removed we are from living with, and being dependent on, animals the better we can afford to care for them as fellow spirits, not just as food in our children's mouths or sources of clothing and shelter.

One of the current issues in my mailbag at the moment is the import of wild birds from Africa. In Britain the keeping of wild birds is regarded as a hobby, a luxury, a diversion. We have to remember that a large percentage of those birds die en route to us. On the other hand, in most of the countries that send wild birds to us the population see them as a source of income, a rare means of earning a precarious living for themselves and for their family. And looking at things from the other end of the telescope helps us to understand why it is sometimes so difficult to achieve our objectives and translate our aim to reduce appalling practices into legislation. What we see as a straightforward plan to ease suffering can be interpreted in some countries as a calculated attempt to deny a family its livelihood. This was one of the arguments we faced when dealing with the ban on the killing of seals.

One of my pleas to members of the RSPCA is that in their lobbying, collectively and individually, whether it be locally, nationally or now internationally – where so much legislation is passed concerning the welfare of the animals and the environment – they must become more sensitive. We sometimes try to cover too many issues too quickly, with the result that we do not get into the detail and we do not concentrate our energies into translating our aims into action.

Let me give you an example. One of the busiest agendas on animal welfare is the monthly meeting in Strasbourg of the intergroup of Members of the European Parliament, led on the Secretariat side by Ian Ferguson. In the last six months they have covered drift netting for tuna and dolphins, cosmetic testing on animals, tropical birds, habitats, bears, patenting of animals, zoos, ivory (elephant and walrus), hunting, dogs, farming practices, sheep, goats, slaughter of animals, poultry, deer, rabbits, game, veterinary inspection, shell fish, fur-bearing animals, tropical forests, animal experiments, donkeys, bulls, horses, hormones and growth promoters, whales, walruses, chimpanzees, monkeys, bees, pigs, cattle, genetic engineering, cats, elephants, seals and greyhounds. Now, missing from that list, you will have noticed, are frogs, geese and the caging of battery hens. Their plight has not actually been raised in the last six months, but I can assure you that they were dealt with in detail in the previous six months.

So you can see the problem which we are up against and which, of course, the RSPCA as an umbrella organisation in the field of animal welfare has to face up to. Everybody expects something to be done about their pet subject. But it should be recognised, and some people sometimes should be reminded, that there is limited scope. This is the harsh reality, whether we like it or not. There is only limited scope for getting time in the parliamentary agenda, whether nationally or internationally, for new legislation on any subject. And any one who has tried to get a Private Member's Bill discussed in Westminster will know just what the pressures are. Consequently, we as Members in the European Parliament have to decide between a number of different courses of action when a specific issue is raised with us: whether, first of all, we can get legislation on a pan-European basis; whether we can merely lobby by raising the issue on the floor of the House and creating a fuss with the Commission and publicly airing the issue, so that the media trumpet it aloud; whether we actually go and lobby an individual national government, if it is a national problem or, indeed, if it is only a regional problem; or indeed, the ultimate extreme, whether we can actually seek and achieve import embargoes on the product concerned, as in the case of seal skins. All this procedure, frustrating for everyone, takes time – and lots of it. My own report on pigs, calves, transport and the caging of battery hens took from 1985 to 1990 to get draft legislation. That is not fast enough for some of the less responsible organisations who have limited understanding of the way things work out, to put no finer point on it, sometimes want maximum publicity in order to swell their coffers and keep their members happy. I dissociate the RSPCA completely from those less-than-responsible organisations, but I am sure that some members will know who they are.

Let me give you an example of how impatience and lack of understanding of the system has in fact been counter-productive – where the lobby actually got it wrong: the recent media coverage of the Draft Commission proposals amending the cosmetics directory. It was suggested in the media that this would lead to increased testing on animals of an existing list of cosmetics. Animal welfare groups wrote to all their members, urging them to write to MEPs to stop this Draft legislation. I had some extremely rude and rough letters telling me what would happen to me if I did not stop this Draft Directive. The average run of letters to me was 300 per week. If you multiply that by 518, the number of Members of the European Parliament, you will see that a small rain forest was destroyed by people just writing on this subject. My reply – and I reply to every single one of the letters sent to me, if they are addressed to me personally and signed by the author – was treated with mockery. I had people writing back to say that I was lying; that, because they had read it in their local paper, their circular, their animal welfare journal, it must, therefore, be true. My own response, a factual reply, based on intense investigation, was rejected. It was rejected because it denied absolutely what the lobbyists were actually saying. There will be no increase in testing on animals. The ambition of an overwhelming majority of Members of the European Parliament is to stop the testing of cosmetics on animals. Full stop. But, frankly, most of the lobby organisations were so busy addressing themselves to this initial draft on what they perceived as an increase in testing, that they actually missed the real issue they should have been lobbying on, which was to stop all testing for cosmetics. It is not actually too late, but it does need to be done much more subtly than it has been in that particular campaign. The lobby on the issue was, in effect, being based on mischief in some cases and actually on make-believe.

My point is this. Successful though the lobby may be in encouraging ordinary people to write to their MEP, it loses its impact and power by leading with a falsehood, and tends merely to put up the backs of precisely the people the lobby seeks to influence.

Now, having outlined one shortcoming in the animal welfare lobby, it is appropriate for me to close by mentioning some successes. A short case study of one of our newer members, Spain, is relevant. When Spain first joined the European Community, I do not believe they had words for animal welfare in their dictionary. It has always been my perception that in Spain a dog was an animal you kept in order to kick when you had an argument with your wife. I know it is always unfair to generalise about any nationality, but that was my general perception. The fact is that since Spain became a Member of the European Community, their MEPs have been invited to, and participated actively in, the intergroup. Secondly, their government Ministers have been subjected to the sort of mass letter-writing campaigns I have been talking about, but mostly on widely justified and soundly based issues. This is the first time a Spanish Minister has ever been lobbied successfully in that field. Now it is an extremely slow process, but I can tell you that Spanish Ministers do not like being embarrassed on the floor of the European Parliament by MEPs getting up and identifying cruel practices in Spain, and slowly, oh so slowly, we are beginning to see some progress in Spain. The laws are beginning to be put in place – if only they would start implementing them.

That is the proof – that one example – that constructive, effective and persistent lobbying does actually work.

Now can I close as I began, by thanking and congratulating the RSPCA. The Society sets an excellent example to others by its work, its skill and its influence. But I am not going to let it get away with just being patronised by me. Inevitably, like Oliver, I am going to ask on behalf of the animal kingdom for *more*. And I really do feel that something really can be achieved in an area that has already been mentioned, the export of horses for slaughter. Can we be absolutely clear about this. Where bloodstock exports are concerned, horses are looked after a darn sight better in transit, I may say, than MEPs are either on trains or in aeroplanes. But there really is considerable scope, I believe, for Britain having a unilateral position, a unilateral law, governing the export of horses for slaughter. It is something we have had for many years, and I know that it goes against the spirit of the Treaty of Rome. I know that it goes against the particular Article on Free Trade. But there are plenty of precedents that can be cited. So that an exception can be made in order to avoid the completely unnecessary traffic in horses which are going for direct slaughter from these islands. This is a proper campaign for the RSPCA and other organisations and for the intergroup to target on. It is actually legislation which is under the spotlight.

20. Painism: The Ethics of Animal Rights and the Environment

Richard D. Ryder

In everyday discussions about the environment the moral argument is often ill-defined or shifts its ground. That is why some clarification seems desirable. Why *should* we care about the environment? Environmentalists are sometimes unclear in their answers to this question. By comparison, the moral principles of animal protection appear to be amply explained.

Can a zebra be said to have rights – or a tree, or a chair, or a mountain, or a galaxy, or a robot? If rights can be ascribed only to some of these, what is it about them that gives them this special status?

The moral circle

It would be nice to imagine the history of moral development as simply an ever-widening moral circle – widening as new classes of sufferers, made more familiar through increased knowledge and mass communication, are drawn into it. Elsewhere, I have argued the merits of this view.[1] We certainly see this trend over the centuries and we see it now with the spread of internationalism and the growing concern for nonhumans. I have explained it by asserting that humans are intrinsically kind as well as cruel. Our compassion, which often motivates (but does not justify) our moral attitudes, tends naturally to extend to cover all suffering things of which we are not afraid. So we accord rights to others of the tribe, the nation, the species and so on.

Many are uneasy about the use of the word 'rights'. Years ago I felt so uneasy about the word myself that I used 'interests' instead, and even went as far as to invent the term 'speciesism'[2] (as a parallel with racism and sexism). Some people, mostly of the older generation, prefer the words 'responsibility' or 'duty'. But these words are merely the other side of the same coin. I have come round to the view that rights are just human inventions and, provided one remembers this, there is little harm in using the word. I do not, incidentally, see very much difference, except journalistically, between the labels 'animal rights' and 'animal welfare'. The yellow press may have associated the former with extremist violence, but ultimately both denote a concern for the suffering of others.

Morality serves a useful psychological function for the individual by making it easier to decide how to behave; reactions are thus accelerated (there is some survival value in this, I would suggest) and the anxiety over decision-making is reduced. Furthermore, a shared moral code will tend to produce a cohesive (and probably cooperative) society. So it is easy to see why all human communities invent some sort of morality. A moral code is to the human mind rather as a program is to a computer and that program must cover our relationship with the environment around us. In the past this relationship has sometimes been based upon animism, or a belief that plants, and even inanimate objects, have some kind of consciousness. Today, science produces no evidence that this is, in fact, the case. Plants may react to a blow, but so does a detonator; reaction in itself is not evidence of sentience. Nevertheless, some environmentalists still occasionally imply that they believe that trees feel or mountains think. Yet, perhaps it is because science has made it seem most unlikely that mountains or plants *are* conscious that we can now move beyond the animist position into building a morality based firmly upon sentience. We are now liberated by science from the awfulness of having to believe that we constantly inflict pain as we eat vegetables or fell trees. We can, for the first time, confidently draw the circumference of our moral circle around consciousness and yet still be able to live comfortably ourselves. Morality has, at last, become a practical proposition.

So the answer to my question 'What is it that can be said to give a zebra rights, but not a chair or a mountain?' is quite simply consciousness or, more precisely, the capacity to feel pain or distress.

May I say straightaway that I am using the phrase 'pain or distress' in a broad sense to cover all negative experiences of any kind, including such things as fear, discomfort, guilt, shame and so on. I am concerned not only with sensations but with negative states associated with the frustration of drives and with mood. I am referring to 'suffering' of any sort.

I know that I can suffer and, although I can never be *certain* that anything else suffers, I tend to take it on trust that others like me suffer in the same way. In the case of nonhuman animals we have several grounds for supporting this view:

1. They often behave much as we do when hurt – they writhe or scream and try to avoid what is hurting them.
2. There are the same survival reasons for pain: namely, the avoidance of dangerous situations.
3. On the assumption that our nervous systems mediate pain and distress, we can observe that other animals have nervous systems which are similar to our own, anatomically, electrically and chemically.

Clearly, as I have argued, these grounds do not exist in the case of chairs or mountains or the planet itself – although, admittedly, the capacity to feel pain may, conceivably, emerge from totally different structures than our own. We simply do not know whether conventional nervous systems are the only possible basis for consciousness.

But why link morality with consciousness at all, and specifically with pain and distress? I believe this is because morality is defined as being *about right and wrong* and, unless one adopts a religious view, right and wrong are *intrinsically* about what is desired and what is avoided. All major psychological theories, going back to Socrates, postulate that animals in general desire happiness, i.e. they seek pleasure (broadly defined) and avoid pain. But just as pain and pleasure underlie all significant theories of behaviour, including Freud's and Skinner's, so they have also formed the bases of *moral* theories for centuries, and one can see, as a psychologist, that other moral aims, such as justice, freedom and equality, are merely means towards the fundamental ends of pleasure and the avoidance of pain. Where moral theory is different from any theory of behaviour, of course, is that it is about what *ought* to be done and not what *is* done. So morality is not about what we do spontaneously and naturally; indeed moral behaviour is often in conflict with our natural impulses. Murder and rape, for instance, may be prompted by natural impulses; this does not make them right.

I would suggest that much of the confusion between morals and theories of behaviour, between what I *ought* to do and what I *want* to do, is that both are concerned basically with pain and pleasure. But this historic confusion, which continues to arise in everyday debate, can be resolved if one defines morality as dealing exclusively with the pains and pleasures of *others* and not of oneself. This means that we should do to others what we believe will give them pleasure and not do to them what we believe will cause them pain. The all-important question is how to define the category 'others', and I propose to define it to cover all things capable of being conscious of pain or pleasure or both; after all, pain is pain and pleasure is pleasure regardless of who or what experiences them. Thus the boundary of the moral circle must be drawn around the edges of such consciousness. Now what I am saying is that a certain amount of pain, for example we will say x units of pain, is equally bad in whatever conscious system it arises – dog, lobster, human or machine, terrestrial or alien.

Giving pleasure, incidentally, seems less of an imperative than not causing pain. Not only does such a morality avoid some of the difficulties of conventional Utilitarianism (which emphasises pleasure), but it feels, intuitively, to be better; experiencing x units of pain seems very much worse than not experiencing x units of pleasure. There may be many pain-pleasure systems within each of us (intellectual pain-pleasure, sensual pain-pleasure, self-esteem pain-pleasure, for example), but in each case the pain end of the dimension seems to carry more weight than the pleasure end. Who, offered the choice between avoiding torture or experiencing the most intense pleasure, would not choose the former? Who would choose an hour of lovemaking, for example, rather than escape from an hour of burning and whipping and electric shock? The masochist might be able to combine the two, of course. But, surely, the most intense pleasure you can imagine – whether it might be a weekend in Disneyland, listening to *Parsifal* at Bayreuth, or having sex with the popstar of your choice, does not match up to avoiding falling into the hands of Saddam Hussein's torturers. The consciousness of pain and the consciousness of pleasure are clearly the bases for morality, whatever their comparative weightings, and because I believe consciousness to be of such central moral importance I will now discuss it briefly.

Consciousness

Perhaps only because it is so difficult a subject, consciousness has recently been linked with the other great mystery – quantum mechanics. When trying to understand both, you get the feeling that you are attempting to pin down shadows. Certainly, there are similarities between the way consciousness works and the happening of quantum events: first, there *may* be a parallel between free will and indeterminacy; secondly, between wave/particle duality and mind/body duality; thirdly, between consciousness itself and the importance of the observer in quantum physics. The main difference between consciousness and quantum events, it seems to me, is that whereas in quantum physics events are not rigidly tied down to time and place, consciousness does seem to be. In the strange world of quantum physics, not only are events probabilistic but there are theories of retro-active causation and causation at a distance: that is to say, causation acting apparently backwards in time and more quickly across space than the speed of light itself.

Yet it has been argued that sub-atomic particles are themselves figments of consciousness – even that before they were discovered they did not exist! Consciousness itself can be compared with light, having both wave and particle qualities and yet being neither. Furthermore it can be seen as an 'emergent' property. Just as a message *emerges* from the alphabetical letters on a page, so consciousness emerges from the cells of the brain. But the paradox here seems to be that 'emergence' itself can be a property of consciousness and, what is more, may depend on the position of the conscious observer. Unless there is a conscious observer there is no message, just letters. Furthermore whether the observer is inside or outside a phenomenon influences whether or not he or she can see it. The same problem applies to morality: what is good or bad depends upon where you stand. I will return to that shortly.

So although there are intriguing similarities between quantum mechanics and consciousness, there seems to me to be a fundamental difference, and it is this: consciousness is anchored in time and space. As far as *my* consciousness is concerned it is anchored to me here and now. Even so-called out-of-body experiences, in dream or illness, leave behind no evidence that consciousness has ever really departed from the individual brain. My consciousness is always in *me*: it cannot be transferred anywhere else – into you or into an elephant or a computer. Information can be transferred but consciousness cannot.

Painism

There appear to be some words missing from the English language. First, we need a word to describe all conscious states that are negative – 'suffering' seems to be the closest. Then we need a word to describe individuals who have the capacity to suffer. 'Sufferent' would be a possible neologism but, defining pain very broadly, I have decided to use 'painient' and 'painism' to denote, respectively, the capacity to feel pain and the principle that morality should be based upon such a capacity. 'Painience' thus means, simply, the condition of being painient. The difficulty with the word 'hedonism' is that it emphasises pleasure. Sentientism (which I have used extensively in the past) refers to the general capacity to feel and so, arguably, could refer to irrelevant feelings or even to sentient beings incapable of experiencing pain at all; that is why I have abandoned it. We need to concentrate, when considering morality, only upon those conscious experiences that are painful or pleasurable, 'physically' or 'mentally'. I am therefore forced to use painience, painient and painism. Painience is thus a part of consciousness but not all of it. But what of pleasure? Can that enter into the painism argument? Yes, it can, but as the negative of pain. Pleasure is recognised as being on the same dimension as pain but of less intensity at its extreme. The pleasures of playing golf in the rain can certainly outweigh the discomforts; it is only at its extreme that pain always outweighs pleasure.

The masochist is sometimes cited as a problem for hedonistic theories. But even the masochist's pain is sought because it brings greater pleasure. The martyr, too, besides hoping for rewards in the afterlife, suffers pain and death for the greater pleasures of adhering to his beliefs and the knowledge of others' acclaim.

Seeing a dead baby bird on the road the other day caused me to reflect on the brief fragment of consciousness that that little corpse represented. That tiny squashed brain had once been a little vessel of low-voltage painience. Where had that consciousness gone? Could it ever reappear elsewhere in the universe? Or is it (like the family of subatomic particles called bosons rather than their cousins, the fermions) a quality which can be created and destroyed? Where will my consciousness be in a hundred years from now? Why is *my* consciousness so anchored in *my* brain? Why is yours in yours? It is this vulnerability and the non-transferable quality of consciousness which should, I believe, influence our attitude towards other animals and our shared environment, and in the following ways:

First, non-painient things (whatever they may be) can be said to have no rights. Their importance lies only in their value to painient beings.

Secondly, all painient individuals, whatever form they may take (whether human, nonhuman, extraterrestrial or the artificial machines of the future, alive or inanimate), have rights.

Thirdly, because consciousness is anchored in each individual, a morality based upon consciousness cannot 'trade-off' the pains or pleasures of one individual against those of another as if the observer was looking down on both from above.

It is this individual-based, pain-based and non-transferable morality that I call *painism*. Painism combines the altruistic hedonism of Peter Singer's position (while rejecting the trade-off of pains and pleasures across individuals associated with his Utilitarianism) with Tom Regan's philosophy of rights (while rejecting his concept of the 'inherent value' of the individual in favour of the more basic criterion of pain).[3] One problem with Utilitarianism is that it argues that ends justify means. So, conceivably, if a clique of sadists experience more pleasure in total than the pain felt by a child they torture, then they are justified in doing this.

But for what other reason am I reluctant to aggregate pains and pleasures across individuals? The answer is that they are part of conscious experience and there exists a barrier between individuals through which consciousness cannot pass. However much I empathise or sympathise with your pain I can never feel that *same* pain. So, if there are a hundred people each suffering x amount of pain, the significant pain score is x and not $100\,x$. If there is one sentient suffering 10 units of pain and one suffering 5 units of pain, the meaningful pain score is 10, not the sum total of 15. In other words the morally significant measure of pain in a group of painients is the maximum felt by any one of them. Someone may say that 'non-trade-off-ability' does not necessarily follow from non-transferability. Well, I would say that conscious events are unlike any other kind of event, and unlike anything else one might want to add up or 'trade-off'. You can aggregate contemporaneous horse races on different race tracks or wars in different centuries, but you cannot aggregate pains or pleasures in different individuals, because anyone *else's* pleasure is not directly experienced and so is not a conscious event. As soon as I consider the consciousness of another it is no longer *that* consciousness. Your pains and my pains are as different as biscuits and bulldozers. They are in separate universes. So aggregations of pains and pleasures *within* an individual are legitimate but *between* individuals are not. Pleasures and pains must be experienced directly before they can be traded off against each other. Only God can aggregate the pains and pleasures of others and only then if he or she can actually feel them. You can, in a sense, add up and compare pains and pleasures in different individuals, but not in a morally meaningful way. Without the *direct experiencing* of pains and pleasures they are not really there – we are merely counting their husks.

What then, briefly, are the implications of painism? I am afraid it undermines those in the Green movement who argue as if hedgerows, ozone layers and tropical rain forests themselves have rights. In the absence of even minimal evidence of their painience, I would say that these things are important only because their survival affects the consciousness of other individuals, human and nonhuman, today and in the future. If consciousness and, in particular, painience come to an end in the universe, then, surely, nothing will matter: the survival of a tropical rain forest will be neither here nor there. Similarly, the survival of a species *per se* does not matter, for species themselves feel nothing. A species's survival *does* matter a great deal, however, in its effects upon the consciousness of its *individual members* and of others not of that species. Causing suffering to an *individual*, whatever the species, is what is wrong, and causing pain to one individual is as bad as causing that same magnitude of pain to many.

One snag of painism is that it appears pacifist and so might seem to prohibit the infliction of even mild pain on an individual in order to prevent him causing far greater pains to others. It might prevent the killing or capture of Hitler in 1942, for instance. But this is a special case, surely. We are dealing with the *agent* of suffering to others and by restraining him we are aiming to reduce that suffering. Removing Hitler is like removing any other source of pain – fire, poverty or disease, for example. It is not like experimenting upon an *innocent* child in order to try to find a cure for others' illnesses, it is like dealing with disease itself. Hitler is not innocent and to this extent has forfeited his rights.

During the 1980s, as a result of our animal protection campaigning, the British government established the principle of calculating cost-benefit analyses under the law. Section 5 of the Animals (Scientific Procedures) Act 1986 requires the Home Secretary to weigh the pain and distress likely to be caused to animals against the benefits likely to result from research performed upon them. This politically important (but theoretically misguided) Utilitarian procedure is now in operation. It follows Singer rather than Regan. However, laws protecting humans, in general, accord more with Regan than Singer. Nor would painism be speciesist in this way – each innocent individual, human or nonhuman, has an absolute right not to be subjected to painful research, regardless of any benefits to others.

The animal protection movement often faces ethical dilemmas in practice. One concerns the choice between allowing *many* animals to suffer mildly or permitting fewer to suffer more *intensely*. The Home Office, for example, has sometimes argued that the total number of animals being used for research could be reduced if the same animals were used for more than one experiment. Painism argues strongly against this and, indeed, the consensus within the animal movement has swung the painist way in recent years in concluding that it is more desirable to reduce the *maximum* levels of suffering in any individual than merely to reduce the *number* of animals suffering.

Environmentalism

There are, I believe, at least seven main motives for being an environmentalist, and five out of the seven are basically anthropocentric. These five motives are concerned with *thrift* (e.g. the conservation of energy and other natural resources for future human use), *aesthetics* (e.g. the protection of animals, countryside and buildings because they are beautiful), *health* (e.g. the campaigns against dangerous radioactive and chemical pollution), *science* (e.g. the protection of rain forests as depositories of species as yet not fully explored by science), and *history* (e.g. the protection of geographical or ethnic features and buildings because of their historical significance).

Although these five categories are all largely anthropocentric, in as much as some refer to a concern for the welfare of future human generations, we can legitimately call them *moral* concerns because they are indeed concerned with the pains and pleasures of *others*, albeit of only one species. But it is the remaining two categories of motive which seem to me to be less speciesist.

The first of these I have called *mystical* and it is characterised by a deep poetic feeling of reverence for nature and, indeed, for the bond which unites human and other animals. Two of the great pioneers of the environmental movement, Ernst Haeckel in Germany and Henry Thoreau in America, were in this category although, sadly, many of their followers veered away from sharing their respect for animals and some, in sentimentally over-emphasising the value of tribal and peasant communities, have perpetuated unnecessary cruelties arguing, for example, that traditional methods of hunting and killing animals should be allowed to continue.

The second motive is *compassion*, and it is close to the mystical, but concentrates far more upon the pain of others which it seeks to alleviate. Admittedly, some environmentalists in this camp talk of trees and rocks as if they, too, had feelings, and this puts their ideas closer to those of animal rights and hedonistic theorists but, seemingly, in defiance of the scientific facts.

The cult of machismo

I believe that inside many environmentalists there is, in reality, a painist trying to get out, but that some are too bashful to admit it, even to themselves. I do not accept the view expressed in some circles that all environmentalists are anthropocentric and selfish and becoming more so. People have hidden and denied their concern for the suffering of others, especially the others of other species, on many grounds and not least because of the pernicious and almost universal influence of the cult of machismo.

When challenged by a threatening bully or by financial problems we can either fight, fly or surrender. Surrendering (giving in) is widely seen, not as diplomacy or tact, but as cowardice or loss of face. Flight, similarly, although sometimes excused if used only as a short-term tactic, is also condemned and on similar grounds. Only fight, whether or not successful, is widely acclaimed.

Machismo is the culturally exaggerated version of this elementary psychological coping , mechanism – the fight response. Of all such mechanisms, it is fight which is the most culturally acclaimed.

This is, I believe, a major flaw not only in European cultures but in many other cultures too. It is at the root of much of the violence, crime and cruelty between individuals and groups in the world today. When there are no real battles to be fought they have to be invented, and so we have violent sports, crime, bull-fighting, fox-hunting, gang warfare, and the rest. I accept that we can all be aggressive without any cultural encouragement. But this innate spark of aggressiveness is constantly being fanned into flames culturally by the inculcated need to prove our bravery and our stoicism on every possible occasion.

Machismo is a deadly disease, and a self-inflicted one. It affects chiefly the male of the species but, increasingly, the female also. It cuts across nearly all we are trying to achieve in the Green movement, bolstering not only racism and sexism but speciesism, and encouraging the view that environmentalism is wet or wimpy. Any attempts to avoid dangers or prevent disease or suffering can strike the macho man as forms of weakness – 'Who's afraid of greenhouse effects or a little pollution? Why, I remember breathing thick *smog* when I was a boy!' Machismo encourages humans to suppress their natural compassion and to pretend that they do not mind killing or inflicting pain. Machismo can drive on the vivisector and intensive farmer no less than the huntsman, trapper, lion-tamer and bull fighter. The cult of so-called manliness has been a feature of aggressive societies of every age; it was a part of Roman culture and, indeed, of Nazism, of the Viking invader and the British Empire-builder.

Machismo is, of course, largely a sham. Men in a crowd appear brave and violent because they are cowards; because they do not dare to be non-violent in front of their peers. They are cruel to animals and destructive of the environment often for the very same reason. I believe we must cast out machismo – it threatens the future of life on this planet. We must not allow the macho mentality to suppress the sensitive, compassionate and caring side which is in every one of us. At home and at school we must stop rewarding stoicism – 'Pull yourself together, old chap. Don't cry – that would never do' – and cease applauding all those bloody and violent sports that boys are forced into. We should have had enough of all that. We must go further; we must suppress the bullies who turn our worst schools into training camps for yobbism; we must reject the machismo of which we see too much among trappers, whalers, badger-baiters, dog-fighters, sealers, forest-fellers, and environmental vandals. To worry about dumping oil and toxic waste in the oceans, to worry about the sufferings of whales, to worry about the emission of CFCs and carbon dioxide are *not* signs of starry-eyed weakness. They are signs of sanity and strength.

Before the development of the Gulf crisis there was much debate about what to do with the huge military forces of East and West after the amazing détente of the late 1980s. What, for example, is to be the role of NATO over the next twenty years? How do you safely occupy hundreds of thousands of men under arms? Surely one answer is to redeploy them to fight the great environmental battles; to cleanse the seas, the land and the air; to reduce nonhuman as well as human suffering. If peace continues, the armies of West and East could plant a million trees a day; build alternative energy factories to use wind, sun or sea; bring food to the starving and protect wildlife. There is so much to be done, which could be well done by disciplined men and women – by a Green army, by environmental commando forces maintaining their fitness and exercising their sophisticated technologies in tough terrains.

Bringing environmentalism and animal welfare together

Some may say I have played down the possible conflicts between environmentalists and animal rightists, and the conflicts between human and nonhuman interests. If I have, it is because I do not believe these conflicts are often very great, or unresolvable, provided we remember that environmentalism ultimately is, when we really think about it, about the reduction or avoidance of suffering. That is to say we are right to want to protect a hillside because its destruction would cause pain to those painients who live on it and to many humans whose aesthetic pleasure would be spoiled. It is the rights of these painients we are protecting.

Sometimes it is alleged that environmentalism and animal rights interests always conflict. This is an exaggeration. But *sometimes* they do. After all, the two movements have different aims: typically, animal rights campaigners are interested in *individuals* while environmentalists are concerned with *species*; the animal rightist is concerned with *suffering* whereas the environmentalist at least pretends *not* to be; and sometimes the environmentalist is concerned only with *human* interests. The answer to these differences is that conflicts between human and nonhuman interests should be tackled with as much care as interhuman disputes are daily addressed in civilised societies. The existence of conflicts does not mean that one side of the argument is totally invalid.

If we can accept that speciesism is as wrong and as irrational as sexism and racism then, perhaps, we can also accept that environmentalism, at bottom, should be motivated by painism – the desire to reduce individual suffering in whatever creatures it happens to occur, human or nonhuman, terrestrial or alien, natural or artificial. I have argued that the conservation of a species is important primarily because we are dealing with the consciousness of each individual member of that species. The conservation of a species may also be important because the awareness of the existence of that species will give pleasure, in the future, to individual members of our own and other species. Furthermore, the continuation of that species may help maintain the so-called balance of nature and have little-understood and currently incalculable benefits for innumerable painient individuals of many species.

In practice environmentalism (unlike consumerism) almost always coincides with animal welfare. The disastrous felling of tropical rain forests in South America, for example, has been largely to feed cruelly-slaughtered cows for the American beefburger industry. One can say, in passing, that worldwide vegetarianism would not only prevent the inhumane rearing and killing of billions of painient individuals each year but would also reduce the clearance of rain forest, human starvation in the Third World, coronaries and cancers in the affluent northern hemisphere and the damaging greenhouse effects of methane.

I can honestly say that after a career of over twenty years as both an environmentalist and an animal rights campaigner I have never experienced a major conflict between the two concerns. Indeed they can help each other, giving mutual assistance, politically and philosophically. Both campaigns can be held together by being based on painism. We must never forget that we are dealing with mountains of pain, often caused unthinkingly for mere human convenience. I believe that all of us in the Green movement are fighting for a great moral revolution – perhaps the most significant change in moral outlook this millennium.

References

1. Richard D. Ryder, *Animal Revolution: Changing Attitudes Towards Speciesism*, Blackwell, 1989
2. Richard D. Ryder, 'Speciesism', leaflet, 1970, and Richard D. Ryder: 'Experiments on Animals' in *Animals, Men and Morals*, ed.

Stanley and Roslind Godlovitch and John Harris, Gollancz, 1971
3. Peter Singer, *Animal Liberation*, second edition, Jonathan Cape, 1990
4. Tom Regan, *The Case for Animal Rights*, Routledge & Kegan Paul, 1983

Index